CELESTIALS

THE EMERGENT SPECIES

#1 BEST SELLING AUTHOR

RANDY LEE HIGGINS, PH.D.

Celestials

Copyright © 2024 by Randy Lee Higgins. All rights reserved.

No part of this book may be used or reproduced in any manner whatsoever without written permission, except in the case of brief quotations embodied in critical articles and reviews. For more information, e-mail all inquiries to info@mindstirmedia.com.

MINDSTIR MEDIA

Published by MindStir Media, LLC

45 Lafayette Rd | Suite 181| North Hampton, NH 03862 | USA

1.800.767.0531 | www.mindstirmedia.com

Printed in the United States of America.

ISBN-13: 978-1-963844-50-4

*This book is to, for and about
Gavin Geoffrey Dillard.*

FOREWORD

We are not alone. We were never alone. Far from it, we are surrounded at every moment of our lives by innumerable "beings" of infinite ilks. Some are guides, "ascended masters," who have gone through the pangs of the physical existences and completed their courses. Most are beings who have yet dared to delve into the quirky oceans of this third-dimensional foray, this cosmic curriculum.

Professor Higgins' ETs seem to be of the latter sort, entities who watch us and await our responses and choices the way we might watch our episodic comedies and dramas. We are a theatrical, an amusement, a conundrum, and perhaps even a source of edification. We are angels who have chosen this exercise, not as a punishment, but as a prize, an honor, a feat of bravery. Indeed, I have often heard it said that the angels envy us, perhaps the way that we envy and "deify" the actors and athletes on our stages and fields.

Randy's seem a feisty bunch, eager and willing to throw in a "No no no, turn left!" when appropriate. When asked. Yes, asked, as there are strict rules regarding interference. After all, these are not humans — they taste the lasagna only through inference — oh, but they do have opinions!

As for our poetic style here, this staccato stream-of-consciousness, it is most unique. I have come to read it as ticker tape, a sort of metaphysic Morse code, brazenly transcribed through the Professor's deft fingers. He truly can't help himself — once that dam is perforated, the river becomes unstoppable.

As for us, the readers — and fellows in this phantasmagorically sentient opera — read with care, follow the flow. After all, the whole cosmos is watching!

~ Gavin Geoffrey Dillard
BLACK MOUNTAIN POEMS, GRAYBEARD
ABBEY, THE COMFORT OF STONE

PART ONE

Things you used to care about –

YOU DON'T CARE ABOUT ANYMORE.

....

One day you will wake up –

And:

NOT QUITE KNOW YOURSELF.

It will be one of those:

"WHO AM I? WHERE AM I?" moments.

You'll likely be remembering an:

UNSETTLING DREAM.

A *LURING* dream.

A TEASING dream.

Hinting...

Challenging –

DARING –

You to remember.

You'll know:

SOMETHING IS UP.

You'll remember:

ADOLESCENCE.

Or THE FIRST TIME YOU LEFT YOUR BODY AND FLEW AROUND THE ROOM.

Or your first taste of FORBIDDEN LOVE.

OR THE DAY YOU MOVED TO CALIFORNIA AND SWORE YOU'D DIED AND GONE TO HEAVEN.

You KNEW –

That the UNIVERSE –

Had PICKED YOU UP.

And DEPOSITED YOU SOME BRAND NEW PLACE OF ITS OWN CHOOSING.

And you DIDN'T MIND AT ALL THE ROUGH AND RUDE BEHAVIOR.

WIDE-EYED –

YOU *YELPED* –

WITH GLEE.

....

You SCARCELY REMEMBERED THE OLD WORLD –

OLD FRIENDS –

OLD…

WAYS.

LET ALONE MISSED THEM.

THERE IS NO TIME FOR MISSING.

REALITY IS:

PRESSING.

AND *URGENT*.

AND DEMANDING.

All your senses must COME TO BEAR.

1000% is required now –

And you are ALL IN.

YOU HAVE NEVER BEEN SURER IN YOUR LIFE.

NOR HAVE YOU BEEN MORE *DUMBFOUNDED*.

You BEHOLD.

You WAIT.

THE ONLY SOUND YOU CAN OFFER IS A *GASP*.

AND YOU KNOW VERY WELL THIS GASP WILL BE

UNDERSTOOD.

This gasp is EXACTLY WHAT YOU MEAN.

YOU KNOW THAT YOU ARE NOT ALONE.

AND YOU KNOW THAT YOU ARE:

MORE UNDERSTOOD THAN YOU HAVE EVER BEEN IN YOUR LIFE.

COULD THIS BE THE FRIEND YOU HAVE BEEN WAITING FOR YOUR ENTIRE LIFE?

There is NO DOUBT.

Only SURETY.

You know that the only thing that is required is that you be your HONEST SELF.

Like a fingerprint.

Or eye recognition biometrics.

You know that NO ONE WOULD QUALIFY –

Could BREAK THE CODE –

But YOU.

YOU DO KNOW DESTINY WHEN YOU SEE IT.

WHEN YOU EXPERIENCE IT.

WHEN YOU –

ARE –

IT.

YOU DON'T THINK YOU HAVE EVER KNOWN A –

SATISFACTION –

SO SWEET.

SO COMPREHENSIVE.

SO COMPLETE.

All that's required is just:

YOU BEING YOU.

YOU COULDN'T GET IT WRONG IF YOU TRIED.

....

How you expect it's going to be –

IS NOT HOW IT'S GOING TO BE.

SURPRISE will be the TOUCHSTONE –

Not:

Planning, figuring out, "getting there."

Not SOLUTIONS.

YOU WILL LEARN FROM MISTAKES.

YOU WILL HAVE A NEW "RULE OF THUMB."

ASK WHAT A HUMAN WOULD DO AND DO THE EXACT OPPOSITE.

ASK *WHAT YOU WOULD HAVE DONE* –

AND DO THE EXACT OPPOSITE.

I am not saying the Apocalypse was a MISTAKE –

ON THE CONTRARY.

BUT YOU WILL LEARN FROM IT.

AND IT WILL BE YOUR TOUCHSTONE NOW.

THE APOCALYPSE WILL BE YOUR TOUCHSTONE.

THE SAME WAY BABY JESUS USED TO BE.

....

But the only baby will be:

YOU –

Now.

You and maybe your cat Roji who turns upside down so you can scratch his neck.

THERE WILL BE NO SHORTAGE OF LOVE.

There will be no shortage of "AAAWWW..."s.

The HEART is the new YARDSTICK.

YOU are the new YARDSTICK.

The new METRIC.

YOU WILL MEASURE REALITIES IN TERMS OF "YOUS."

YOU WILL MEASURE TIME IN TERMS OF "YOUS."

YOU WILL MEASURE EPOCHS IN TERMS OF "YOUS."

YOU WILL MEASURE LIGHTYEARS IN TERMS OF "YOUS."

You will say things like:

"How may MES does it take to change a light bulb?"

OR:

"HOW MANY MES DOES IT TAKE TO PASS A PIECE OF LEGISLATATION?"

OR:

"HOW MANY BILLIONS OF MES HAVE TO BE SLAUGHTERED BEFORE WE DECIDE THAT'S NOT WHAT WE WANT TO BE DOING?

OR:

"HOW MANY MES DO WE NEED TO SEND INTO OUTER SPACE BEFORE WE REALIZE WE CAN DO THE SAME THING AND EVEN BETTER BY LYING ON OUR BED AND *GOING DEEP* –

OR DREAMING?"

"HOW MANY MES WILL IT TAKE TO FIGURE OUT THAT WE ARE LOVE AND LIGHT AND SO WE'D BETTER GET TO OUR BUSINESS OF *DOING* LOVE AND LIGHT?

LIVING LOVE AND LIGHT?

BEING LOVE AND LIGHT?

....

And yet we know –

OH YES WE KNOW:

ONE IS ENOUGH.
IF THERE IS ME –
THAT IS ENOUGH.
ENLIGHTENMENT IS NOT A MASS EVENT.
CREATING REALITIES IS NOT A MASS EVENT.
YOU CAN SAY IT IS, BUT IT REALLY ISN'T.
ONE IS PLENTY.
ONE:
PERSON:
CAN DO IT ALL.
....
ONE PERSON CAN START AN EPOCH.
AN ERA.
A PLANET.
AN EON.
AN AGE:
A:
GALACTIC UNDERTAKING.
WITH ALL THE BLESSINGS NECESSARY.
WITH ALL PERMISSIONS GRANTED.
WITH THE FULL BACKING OF BOTH ANCIENT HISTORY AND THE:
INTERGALACTIC FEDERATION.
THE LIGHT IS GREEN.
THE STARS ARE ALL ALIGNED.
THE LOINS ARE FULL TO BURSTING.
THE SHIPS HAVE ARRIVED.
THE BLACKBOARD IS:
WIPED.

THERE IS NO OPPOSITION.

THE TRAVELLERS ARE READY TO:

ARRIVE.

....

It will not feel as though you died.

It will be like you wake up late one morning –

And you dreamily remember that you're going to be starting school soon.

You don't mind.

You like school.

You do well in school.

You make friends easily.

You're sure you'll see many of the friends you already know.

You know it will be –

RELATIVELY –

Easy.

You're smart.

The teachers like you.

The teachers know your family.

Your "position" is secure.

Being teacher's pet will be a piece of cake.

This is not bragging –

Not ego –

Just KNOWLEDGE.

Just ACCURATE ASSESSMENT OF THE LAY OF THE LAND.

Your heart is natively generous.

Your INTELLIGENCE is generous.

YOU KNOW THAT YOUR WORLD –

AND OTHER PEOPLE –

AND TREES AND SQUIRRELS AND SUNSHINE AND RAINBOWS AND STARS –

SHOW YOU WHO YOU ARE.

They are your ARRAY –

Of incarnations.

THEY PLEASE YOU.

And you know that the people –

AND TREES AND SQUIRRELS AND SUNSHINE AND RAINBOWS AND STARS –

Are *HAPPY TO HAVE YOU AS AN INCARNATION OF THEM!*

There is no embarrassment WHATSOEVER –

That your life is an inclusive MUTUAL ADMIRATION SOCIETY.

When you watch the news –

YOU SAY THE SAME THING!

"I know you! I know you! I know you! There you are!"

WHEN YOU LOOK UP AT THE SUN –

OR INTO THE NIGHT SKY –

YOU SAY THE SAME THING!

"I KNOW YOU! THERE YOU ARE!"

....

You remember breaking out of a dinosaur egg.

Learning to flap your wings.

You were an adorable PTERADACTYL.

YOU KNEW YOU DID YOUR PARENTS PROUD.

How proudly you flew in those prehistoric skies.

How proudly you killed.

How proudly you died.

EVEN AS A FOSSIL –

MILLIONS OF YEARS LATER –

YOUR BEAUTY –

YOUR *JOY* –

IS UNMISTAKABLE.

IT LIVES ON IN YOU STILL.

And even as a HUMAN.

YOU DID WHAT YOU DID.

YOU EXCELLED IN ALL THE IMPORTANT WAYS.

YOU EXPERIENCED EVENTS THAT WERE *DEEMED* MISTAKES –

BUT WERE ACTUALLY REQUIRED CURRICULA.

THEY *MADE YOU WHO YOU WERE.*

Even your TRAGEDIES were *EPIC.*

You remember the wars.

You remember the rivalries.

Silly in retrospect.

AND YET EACH DROP OF BILE WAS A *REQUIREMENT.*

NECESSARY.

YOU HAD TO BE WHO YOU HAD TO BE WHO YOU HAD TO BE.

THERE WAS NO ESCAPING.

The script was seared into your DNA and there was no backing out.

SELF-HATRED DID NOT DIMINISH THOSE QUALITIES IN THE LEAST BUT MERELY REINFORCED THEM.

TRY AS YOU MIGHT:

YOU COULD NOT ESCAPE YOURSELF.

NOR COULD YOU ESCAPE YOUR:

TEEMING, *SWARMING* INCARNATIONS.

They kept you DIZZY with their RELENTLESS PUMMELING.

They would not STOP.

THEY WOULD NOT SHUT UP.

YOU WOULD NOT SHUT UP.

IT WAS LIKE A BABY THAT *HAD TO* BE BORN.

AN ORGASM THAT *HAD TO* BE SHOT.

NO WAS NOT AN OPTION.

WHAT YOU HAD TO DO WAS WHAT YOU HAD TO DO AND THERE WAS NO GETTING OUT OF IT.

YOU –

HAD –

TO BE:

YOU.

And you were.

And eventually…

AFTER MORE DEATHS AND MORE KILLINGS THAN COULD EVEN BE TALLIED –

OR REMEMBERED…

YOU LEARNED TO:

LOVE –

YOURSELF.

Well…

It was a KIND OF COMPASSION.

YOU ULTIMATELY DID:

BREAK YOUR OWN HEART.

SEEING YOUR SUFFERING.

THAT MOMENT –
THAT GASP –
OF SELF-AWARENESS.
YOU:
SAW:
YOURSELF.
AND YOUR HEART BROKE.
AT THE SIGHT OF YOU.
THAT WAS THE BEGINNING.
THAT WAS –
ULTIMATELY –
THE BEGINNING –
OF THE:
GRADUATAION.
THE GRADUATION FROM HUMANITY.
....
There is a:
HIGHER KIND OF BEING.
GOD-LIKE.
ANGELIC.
INTERGALACTIC.
CAPABLE OF:
LOVING:
EVERYTHING.
BECAUSE IN EVERYTHING:
IT SEES:
ITSELF.
THAT IS A NEW KIND OF BEING.

WHEN THE HEART OPENS…
YOU LOOK UP –
AND YOU SEE LIGHT.
AND THE LIGHT CASCADES DOWN ON YOU LIKE A:
TSUNAMI.
AND IT BRINGS WITH IT:
AN INTERSTELLAR –
INTERDIMENSIONAL:
OMNISCIENCE.
YOU *KNOW* EVERYTHING.
BECAUSE YOU –
ARE –
EVERYTHING.
YOU:
ARE:
EVERYONE.
EVERY STAR.
EVERY WARMONGER.
EVERY CAVEMAN CHEWING ON *SOMEBODY'S* LEG –
BLOOD AND FAT DRIPPING OFF YOUR CHIN.
IT BREAKS YOUR HEART AND YOU SAY:
YES.
YOUR HEART BREAKS.
OVER AND OVER AND OVER AND OVER AGAIN.
IT SHATTERS.
TO SMITHEREENS.
YOUR HEART:
BECOMES:

OPEN SKY.
YOUR HEART BECOMES:
DEEP SPACE.
HOLDING EVERYTHING –
WITHOUT GRASPING.
HOLDING BY:
LETTING GO.
RESISTING NOTHING.
SMILING AT EVERYTHING.
CRYING AT EVERYTHING.
RECOGNIZING –
EVERYTHING –
AS:
WHO YOU ARE.
YOU DON'T MIND THE:
INDIGNITY.
No.
Every INDIGNITY –
Is WELCOMED.
THE GRAVER THE INDIGNITY –
THE GREATER THE COMPASSIONATE EMBRACE.
ALL IS HUGGED TO YOUR HEART.
SO CLOSE…
YOU FEEL THEIR HEART BEATING INTO YOURS.
UNTIL:
THEY MERGE.
NOW *THEIR* HEART –
IS BEATING IN:

YOUR CHEST.
And now you:
SMILE.
You say:
YES.
And you *MEAN:*
YES.
IT TOOK A LOT TO GET HERE.
BUT YOU WOULDN'T WANT TO BE ANYWHERE ELSE.
YOU ARE EXACTLY WHERE YOU WANT TO BE.
AND YOU:
ARE:
EVERYWHERE.

PART TWO

You won't recognize yourself.

Well, you will and you won't.

Everything will be the SAME –

AND YET EVERYTHING WILL BE ABSOLUTELY UNRECOGNIZABLE.

Nothing will be where it was before.

AND LOTS OF THINGS WILL BE THERE THAT YOU'VE NEVER SEEN BEFORE.

But there will be a GENTLENESS to it.

I THINK THE MAIN THING THAT WILL BE FAMILIAR WILL IN FACT BE THE GENTLENESS OF EVERYTHING.

YOU HAVE LEARNED TO:

HOLD YOURSELF THROUGH HELL.

The gentleness you NOW EXPERIENCE –

Is YOUR OWN.

The BIGGEST SHIFT OF ALL, perhaps –

Is that LIFE is now simply:

YOU WRIT LARGE.

You look up into the sky –

WHICH YOU DO OFTEN! –

AND YOU SEE YOUR OWN FACE UP THERE.

SMILING.

WHAT A SWEET FACE.

SMILING *AT YOU.*

You learned long ago:

LIFE WILL TREAT YOU THE SAME WAY THAT YOU TREAT YOURSELF.

So you learned long ago the –
WISDOM –
The KINDNESS –
Of BEING NICE TO YOURSELF.
Even when you were a Hun –
Or a Viking –
Or a Roman –
Or a Nazi –
Or an American –
SLAUGHTERING WHOLE PEOPLES –
SLAUGHTERING WHOLE *CONTINENTS* –
OF PEOPLES –
You said –
To *YOURSELF:*
"Hey. I get it. Come here.
Let me hug you.
Can you feel my heart BEATING INTO YOURS?
It's OK. Don't worry. I got you."
And now you are reaping the benefits of that kindness.

....

You have to become a SAINT –
To YOURSELF.
YOU HAVE TO LOVE EVERY UGLY THING ABOUT YOURSELF.
And make it BEAUTIFUL.
YOUR *LOVE* MAKES IT BEAUTIFUL.
Your love for YOURSELF –
Makes YOU beautiful.
Your love for everyone makes THEM beautiful.

YOUR LOVE FOR THE WORLD MAKES THE WORLD BEAUTIFUL.

YOU KNOW HOW TO DO THAT NOW AND ISN'T THAT A MARVEL?

It's just where you are now.

It's the GRADE you're in.

You do feel ON TOP OF THE WORLD –

AND THAT'S A GOOD FEELING.

But you look down the CORRIDORS –

Of this CAVERNOUS –

INTERGALACETIC –

ACADEMY.

And you are honestly THRILLED –

BY YOUR OWN SMALLNESS.

YOU ARE GLIMPSING *WONDERFUL* TO THE POWER OF INFINITY.

You don't quite have the EYES to see it all yet.

But you feel those eyes BUDDING.

The EARS.

The FINGERS.

THE:

SONGS.

....

The APOCALYPSE was a test.

AND YOU PASSED WITH FLYING COLORS.

You remember it being DRILLED INTO YOUR HEAD:

THE WORLD HAD TO BE DESTROYED TO SHOW YOU THAT IT NEVER EXISTED IN THE FIRST PLACE.

You remember the SHOCK and THRILL when you first heard that.

THAT WAS THE BEGINNING OF YOU GRASPING --

BEYOND HUMAN INTELLIGENCE.

Not just "LIFE BEYOND DEATH" –

ALTHOUGH YES THAT TOO!

But:

LIFE BEYOND HUMAN.

LIFE BEYOND EARTH.

LIFE BEYOND PHYSICAL REALITY.

LIFE BEYOND TIME.

LIFE BEYOND 3D.

LIFE BEYOND THE SPACETIME CONTINUUM.

LIFE BEYOND THOUGHT.

Once you CAUGHT –

ONCE YOU *GRASPED* –

That GLIMPSE –

IT REALLY WAS LIKE A CASCADE OF DOMINOS AT THAT POINT.

EVERY DOOR IN THE HEAVENS OPENED ALL AT ONCE.

SUN AFTER SUN AFTER SUN AFTER SUN –

BLASTING THROUGH WINDOW AFTER WINDOW AFTER WINDOW AFTER WINDOW.

ALL THE WAY UP TO THE:

BLINDING LIGHT OF WHO YOU KNOW THAT YOU ARE.

Yes.

That was the day:

YOU BECAME YOU.

Everything is the same –

AND YET NOTHING IS EVER THE SAME AGAIN AFTER THAT.

NOTHING.

....

Life got quite a bit SIMPLER –

After that.

Easier.

Instead of sharpening pencils and performing drills –

Now you simply:

BLAST.

YOU FINALLY LEARN THE *ADVANCED LESSON*:

IT DOESN'T MATTER WHAT YOU SAY OR DO.

IT REALLY DOESN'T.

MORALS, EXPECTATIONS, LAWS.

NO.

ALL OF THAT GETS TOSSED IN THE GARBAGE HEAP.

IT DOESN'T MATTER WHAT YOU DO AND IT DOESN'T MATTER WHAT ANYBODY ELSE DOES EITHER.

YOU REALLY JUST DON'T CARE.

WHATEVER YOU DO –

WHATEVER THEY DO –

YOU HOLD IT.

WELL...

WHATEVER YOU DO –

WHATEVER THEY DO:

YOU:

BLAST IT.

YOU BLAST IT WITH THE LIGHT THAT YOU ARE.

YOU PASSED THAT COURSE WITH FLYING COLORS

TOO.

IT REALLY –

TRULY –

AND CATEGORICALLY:

DOESN'T MATTER –

WHAT YOU SAY OR DO.

WHAT MATTERS –

AND THE ONLY THING THAT MATTERS –

IS:

WHAT YOU:

ARE.

AND WHAT YOU:

ARE:

IS:

BLASTING LIGHT.

....

Lately you've been hearing an odd phrase.

"BEYOND LOVE."

YOU UNDERSTAND THAT THE SCANDALOUS SOUND OF THAT IS INTENTIONAL.

THAT'S HOW THEY TEACH YOU.

THEY:

PIQUE –

YOUR SENSIBILITIES –

WHICH THEY KNOW ARE –

ALMOST PAINFULLY REFINED AT THIS POINT.

You're a bit like the PRINCESS AND THE PEA.

EVERY BIT OF INDIGESTION IN ANY FLEA OR AMOBA IS URGENTLY FELT IN YOUR OWN NERVOUS SYSTEM.

SO…
"BEYOND LOVE" –
WHAT WOULD THAT MEAN?
YOU DO TRUST THE "HIGHER UPS."
THEY HAVE WON YOUR TRUST OVER THE EONS.
YOU BEGIN TO WONDER –
SUSPECT –
FEAR –
WORRY:
IS THIS:
BLAST OF LIGHT –
THAT YOU NOW:
ARE –
FATAL?
AND NOW THE –
INTRIGUE –
BEGINS TO PERCOLATE –
FESTER –
WORK ITS WAY INTO YOUR:
THEOLOGICAL MEANDERINGS.
IS THIS:
FATAL –
BLAST OF LIGHT –
THAT YOU:
ARE:
YOUR:
GIFT –
TO THE WORLD?

....

You will have to get used to:

EVERY CELL IN YOUR BODY –

AND EVERY MOLECULE IN YOUR ENVIRONMENT –

BEING *INFUSED WITH BLISS.*

You remember your first out-of-body experience.

IT WAS ECSTATIC.

THROBBING.

SURGING.

THESE ENERGY RUSHES *WHOOSHING* INSIDE YOU –

AND *WHOOSHING* YOU ALL AROUND.

EVERYTHING GLOWED –

INCLUDING YOU!

EVERYTHING WAS *ALIVE* –

INCLUDING YOU! –

AND THROBBING –

SURGING –

WITH CONSCIOUSNESS.

THE WORLD WAS ALIVE.

INTELLIGENT.

EVERYTHING WAS A:

GOD.

INCLUDING YOU!

YES.

THAT'S WHAT YOU'RE GOING TO HAVE TO GET USED TO.

....

Notice.

THIS ISN'T DETERMINED –

OR AFFECTED –

BY CIRCUMSTANCE.

WORLD WAR III CAN BE EXPLODING OVER YOUR HEAD AND *THE THROB OF BLISS WILL* BE UNDETERRED.

SOMEONE CAN BE PICKING YOU UP OVER THEIR HEAD AND BODY SLAMMING YOU ON THE FLOOR –

AND EVERY CELL OF YOUR BODY –

EVERY MOLECULE OF THAT ASSAULT –

WILL BE SINGING THE HALLALUJAH CHORUS –

BOOMING THAT ANGELIC CHOIR.

SLAUGHTER HOUSES CAN BE RUNNING RIVERS OF BLOOD.

BASIC HUMAN RIGHTS CAN BE GETTING *RIPPED* –

FROM ONE DISENFRANCISED GROUP AFTER ANOTHER –

IN CASCADING DOMINOS OF GLOBAL FASCISM.

CANCER CAN BE RAVAGING YOUR BODY –

OR THE BODY OF A LOVED ONE.

THE ANGELIC CHORUSES *STILL DO SCREAM*.

One day your physicists will include *THROBBING SCREAMING BLISS* as a NATURAL LAW.

And yet …

And yet …

AND YET –

BECOMING AWARE OF THE THROBBING SCREAMING BLISS –

IS:

CORRECTIVE.

This is where the OBSERVER SELF has true and profound

PRACTICAL APPLICATIONS.

BECOME AWARE OF YOURSELF BECAUSE *THIS IS WHAT YOU ARE NOW.*

SELF-AWARENESS IS THE DRIVING FORCE BEHIND THIS *EVOLTIONARY LEAP.*

Listen closely:

YOUR –

WORLD –

MERELY –

SIMPLY –

SHOWS YOU –

WHO –

AND WHAT –

YOU ARE.

THE MOST DEFINING ATTRIBUTE OF THIS NEW AGE WILL BE THE:

COMMONIZATION –

OF MIRACLES.

How Randy experiences it is:

LIGHTNING STRIKING ALMOST CONTINUOUSLY.

THERE WILL BE A PROLIFERATION OF SIMULATAENOUS LIGHTNING STRIKES IN EVERY CORNER OF YOUR WORLD.

BUT THE NUMBER ONE –

PRIMARY –

MAGNETIC –

LIGHTNING ROD –

WILL BE:

YOUR OWN BODY.

YOUR OWN:

LIFE.

So yes.

YOUR RIGHTS WILL GET TAKEN AWAY –

AND YET YOU WILL EXPERIENCE YOURSELF BEING FREER BY FAR THAN EVER.

YOUR CANCER DIAGNOSIS WILL BECOME:

A FALSE POSITIVE.

THE MAN WHO THREW YOUR BODY LIKE A RAG DOLL –

WILL DROP TO HIS KNEES –

TEARS STREAMING DOWN HIS FACE –

BEGGING YOUR FORGIVENESS.

WORLD WAR III WILL BE THE:

NECESSARY *PRECIPITATORY CATALYST* –

FOR THE *REINCARNATION* –

OF YOUR PLANET.

ALL DEATHS –

INCLUDING SLAUGHTERS –

WILL BE *RITUAL CURRICULAR GRADUATIONS* –

TO HIGHER, GRANDER, MORE EXPANSIVE ARENAS OF FULFILLMENT.

HIGHLY SOUGHT AFTER *OPPORTUNITIES FOR ADVANCEMENT*.

FOR BOTH THE KILLED AND THE KILLER.

SQUEAMISHNESS WILL BE REPLACED BY:

SCREAMING HALLALUJAH CHORUSES.

The new MOTTO will be:

BE WHOEVER THE FUCK YOU ARE AND DO WHATEVER THE FUCK YOU'RE DOING.

....

The trick?

THAT WORLD –

AND THIS WORLD –

ARE THE SAME.

THAT –

WORLD –

IS HERE:

NOW.

....

OK.

Here we come to an interesting "problem."

SOMETIMES –

YOU WILL FIND YOURSELF:

MORE HAPPY THAN YOU KNOW WHAT TO DO WITH.

INCREASINGLY:

YOU WILL BE MORE HAPPY THAN YOU KNOW WHAT TO DO WITH.

Don't worry.

The Powers That Be –

WILL HELP YOU THROUGH IT.

They will TEACH YOU –

They will EXPLAIN IT TO YOU –

THEY WILL DRAW DIAGRAMS AND CHARTS DETAILING:

How:

WHEN EVERY CELL OF YOUR BODY TURNS ON LIKE A LIGHT BULB –

AND EVERY MOLECULE OF YOUR WORLD TURNS ON LIKE A LIGHT BULB –

AND SINCE LIGHT IS THE *HIGHER DIMENSIONAL* EQUIVALENT OF *JOY* –

Well…

IT CAN'T BE HELPED.

JOY IS A SIDE EFFECT OF:

YOU BEING YOU.

……..

And you see…

The PARAMETERS of SPIRITUAL GROWTH –

Have been REDEFINED.

FORGET ABOUT JESUS.

FORGET ABOUT THE BUDDHA.

FORGET ABOUT QUAN YIN.

EVEN FORGET ABOUT ETS.

THE ONLY "LABEL" THAT MEANS *ANYTHING* NOW IS:

YOU.

Not only are YOU the STANDARD BEARER –

YOU ARE THE *STANDARD*.

You are the YARDSTICK.

You are the GOLD STANDARD.

IF IT'S YOU, IT'S RIGHT.

AND IF IT'S NOT YOU –

Well…

THE THING IS:

YOU ARE EVERYTHING NOW.

SO THERE IS NOTHING THAT *ISN'T* YOU.

I guess what I mean is:

YOU HAVE TO BE THE ONE TO SAY:

IT IS I.

THIS IS ME.

THIS IS RIGHT BECAUSE THIS IS ME.

I guess what I'm saying is:

EVERY NEW DEVELOPMENT WILL:

NEED YOUR APPROVAL.

But the thing is:

YOU APPROVE OF EVERYTHING NOW.

BECAUSE YOUR WORLD IS THE SPONTANEOUS EXPRESSION OF:

YOU --

(Thank you, Patanjali!) –

YOU LOOK INTO THAT MIRROR AND EXCLAIM:

"DAMN! AREN'T I ASTONISHING!"

There is nothing in that WORLD-MIRROR THAT YOU DON'T:

CHERISH.

YOU CHERISH IT –

YOU CHERISH *ALL* OF IT –

BECAUSE *ALL OF IT*:

IS YOU.

YOUR LOVE IS GOING TO BE THE UNDOING OF YOU.

……..

You are going to have to get COMFORTABLE –

With HYPERSPACE.

REALITIES WITHIN REALITIES.

SELVES WITHIN SELVES.

FRACTALING –

IN EVERY DIMENSIONAL DIRECTION ALL AT ONCE.

YOU'RE GOING TO HAVE TO GET USED TO THE INHERENTLY PSYCHEDELIC NATURE OF ALL REALITIES.

THERE IS NOT A "SANE" REALITY AND THEN ALL OTHERS ARE "INSANE."

THEY ARE ALL INSANE.

AND THAT IS THEIR SANITY.

THE ONLY CONSTANT IN THE UNIVERSE IS:

YOU.

WHOEVER YOU ARE IS WHAT IS RIGHT.

AND YOU ARE EVERYTHING.

BUT THIS IS NOT A GENERIC EVERYTHING.

THIS IS *YOU* AS EVERYTHING.

IT IS ALL YOU.

ALWAYS YOU.

NOTHING BUT:

YOU.

THERE IS NOTHING THAT YOU:

AREN'T.

AND YOU LOVE IT ALL!

THE REASON YOU LOVE IT ALL IS THAT:

IT IS ALL YOU –

AND YOU LOVE YOURSELF.

AND THE REASON YOU LOVE YOURSELF IS THAT:

YOU ARE LOVE.

THE WORLD IS LOVE.

LOVE IS THE ONLY THING THERE IS.

Well…

LOVE IS THE ONLY THING THERE IS *NOW.*

GRASP THIS INSANE PSYCHEDELIC LOONEY TUNES FACT AND YOU WILL KNOW:

THE SECRET OF LIFE:

THE REASON THE WORLD IS LOVE IS BECAUSE:

YOU LOVE IT.

YOU PUT THE LOVE THERE.

YOU COULDN'T HELP IT.

THAT'S JUST WHO YOU ARE.

THIS IS NOT ABOUT MORALITY.

THIS IS ABOUT:

YOU BEING IN LOVE.

....

ENTER THE CONUNDRUM.

OK.

WE TALK ABOUT THE SELF.

BUT THE THING IS –

THERE ISN'T REALLY A SELF.

WHAT THERE IS –

IS A BLACK HOLE.

YOU COULD CALL IT THE VOID –

BUT IT IS A *DYNAMIC* VOID.

THIS VOID GAVE BIRTH TO ALL UNIVERSES.

ALL MULTIVERSES.

ALL OMNIVERSES.

ALL ANTIVERSES.

THAT:

BLACK;

HOLE:

IS:

WHO:

YOU:

ARE.

FROM THIS BLACK *HOLE THAT YOU ARE* –

YOU SPEW SELVES.

INFINITIES OF THEM.

THEY ARE ALL PRECIOUS.

THEY ARE ALL YOU.

THEY ALL SUFFER AND DIE OR WHATEVER SELVES DO.

THEY ALL ARE PERFECT.

EVEN IN THEIR SUFFERING AND DYING –

THEY ARE PERFECT.

YOU BLESS THEM ALL.

YOU CHERISH THEM ALL.

NOTHING IS WRONG WITH ANY OF THEM.

AND HERE'S A DOOZY FOR YOU:

BECAUSE ALL OF THESE SELVES –

INCLUDING *YOU!* –

ALWAYS GETS EVERYTHING YOU WANT –

WITHOUT EVEN TRYING –

WITHOUT SO MUCH AS LIFTING A FINGER –

THE ENTIRE *CONCEPT* –

OF *FREE WILL* –

IS NULL AND VOID.

RENDERED IRRELEVANT.

OBSOLETE.

A CHILD'S MYTH LIKE THE EASTER BUNNY.

THERE IS NO RIGHT AND WRONG.

THERE IS ONLY:

PERFECTION.

AND THE REASON THERE IS ONLY PERFECTION IS THAT:

YOU ARE PERFECT –

AND EVERYTHING IS YOU.

THERE ARE NO MORE BAD GUYS.

THERE CANNOT BE ANY MORE BAD GUYS.

BECAUSE IF THERE *WERE* ANY BAD GUYS –

THEY WOULD BE *YOU*.

AND WE KNOW NOW –

THAT YOU ARE NOT BAD.

AND LET THIS SINK IN.

YOU WILL HAVE TO GET USED TO THIS.

BECAUSE YOU ARE PERFECT –

AND EVERYONE IS SIMPLY ANOTHER INCARNATION OF YOU –

AND BECAUSE YOUR WORLD –

ALL OF YOUR WORLDS –

ARE SIMPLY MIRRORS –

SHOWING YOU:

WHO AND WHAT YOU ARE:

THERE REALLY –

AND TRULY –

AND BEYOND ALL DOUBT OR EXCEPTION:

THERE REALLY *ARE* NO:

BAD PEOPLE.

OR BAD EVENTS.

ONLY YOU.

ONLY:

CHERISHABLE.

PRICELESSNESS.

BABY JESUS –

A *BABY LAMB* –

TO THE POWER OF INFINITY.

THAT IS THE DEFINITION OF EVERY INHABITANT –

OF EVERY WORLD –

OF YOURS.

YOU ARE GOING TO HAVE TO GET USED TO THAT.

YOU ARE GOING TO HAVE TO GET USE TO THERE BEING MORE LOVE THAN YOU KNOW WHAT TO DO WITH.

....

Learn to notice the NUZZLES.

FIREWORKS ARE FUN –

BUT LEARN TO APPRECIATE THE KISSES.

THE CARESSES.

THE WHISPERS.

THE "I KNOW YOU!"S.

THE HAND HOLDING.

THE LOVE LETTERS.

FROM YOUR *EXTERNAL SELF.*

You know the model.

From Yogananda and others.

LIFE IS A MOVIE PROJECTOR.

THE SELF IS THE LIGHT.

THE FILM IS THE CONTENTS OF YOUR CONSCIOUSNESS.

THE WORLD IS THE BLANK SCREEN YOU PROJECT ONTO –

SHOWING YOU WHO AND WHAT YOU ARE.

BUT WHAT ABOUT WHEN YOUR WORLD BECOMES *ALIVE?*

ALIVE WITH *YOUR CONSCIOUSNESS?*

WANTING TO ENGAGE YOU?

WANTING TO –

BESTOW –

UNTO YOU?

WANTING TO –

FLIRT –

WITH YOU?

You could say this is a MATERIALIZTION OF YOUR RELATIONSHIP WITH YOUR SELF.

AND IT IS.

BUT IT IS ALSO:

YOUR RELATIONSHIP WITH YOUR SELF.

It is the relationship between your self and your SELF.

Your GREATER SELF and your "personal" self.

THE SELF IN THE WORLD AND THE SELF IN YOUR BODY.

This is where you truly do escape from *SOLIPSISM*.

The fact is:

YOU DO NOT KNOW WHO YOU ARE.

I mean:

YOU WILL ALWAYS BE SURPRISING YOURSELF.

I am saying that there is an:

INDEPDENDENT AGENT.

And yes this independent agent is YOU.

BUT THIS IS A YOU THAT YOU DON'T EXACTLY KNOW.

Sooner or later you will need to grasp that the CELESTIAL –

Is a COLLECTIVE.

Not a SOLITARY SELF.

It is an INTERACTVE SELF.

It is a CHAOTIC SELF.

It is a MULTIDIMENSIONAL SELF.

IT IS A SELF IN WHICH EVERY PERMUTATION OF ITSELF MUST BE EXPLORED IN FULL.

NOT A NEAT AND TIDY PACKAGE.

You will become TOLERANT OF YOUR SELF.

YOUR *SELVES*.

You will stop judging.

You will stop blaming.

You will stop WANTING YOUR SELF TO BE SOMETHING OTHER THAN WHAT IT IS.

You will stop EXPECTING YOUR SELF TO DO SOMETHING OTHER THAN WHAT IT IS DOING.

THIS DOES REQUIRE YOUR HEART TO OPEN THE SIZE OF THE GRAND CANYON.

WIDER THAN THE GALACTIC ARC.

YOU WILL NEED TO BEGIN FINDING A HOME IN DEEP SPACE.

ASTROPHYSICS WILL BECOME THE NEW LANGUAGE OF THE SOUL.

……..

As big as the Universe is:

YOU WILL HAVE TO BE BIGGER.

As big as your SELF is:

YOU WILL HAVE TO BE BIGGER.

YOU AND YOUR SELF WILL CONSTANTLY BE UPPING EACH OTHER.

OUTDOING EACH OTHER.

THIS IS NOT YOU STANDING IN FRONT OF A MIRROR.

THIS IS YOU STANDING IN FRONT OF A MANIAC.

.....

A BEYOND-GENIUS-LEVEL WIZARD OF NECROMANCY.

A PIRATE OF PLANETS.

A MASTER OF DISGUISES.

A PANOPLY OF PERSONALITIES.

A SCHMORASBOARD OF SPECIES.

AN ELOCUTIONER OF HYPERDIMENSIONAL LINGUISTICS.

A NEARLY PSYCHOPATHIC PRANKSTER.

TEASER.

FLIRT.

A KITTEN.

THE KISS OF A BUTTERFLY.

TEARS STREAMING DOWN YOUR CHEEKS AND YOU DON'T KNOW WHY.

GUT-WRENCHING CONVULSIVE SOBBING THAT YOU CAN'T STOP.

You see:

YOU MAY HAVE GRADUATED BUT THE CURRICULA DO NOT CEASE.

THE CAVERNOUS HALLS OF THIS ACADEMY *REALLY*

ARE BIG ENOUGH FOR *ALL OF YOU*.
BOTH THE BIGNESS OF YOU –
AND THE *MULTITUDES* OF YOU.
THE BIGGNESS OF YOU –
AND THE LITTLENESS –
THE *MICROSCOPICNESS* –
OF YOU.
YOU WILL LEARN:
NEVER TO:
EXPECT YOURSELF:
TO BE LESS THAN:
EVERYTHING.

PART THREE

You are in a whole new world now.
You do quite feel like that baby dinosaur
Breaking out of that egg.
Your eyes hurt a bit from the light.
And the air on your new skin does produce a shiver.
BUT YOUR CERTITUDE –
YOUR *URGENCY* –
DOES TAKE PRECIDENCE.
YOU ARE ALIVE AND YOU INTEND TO STAY THAT WAY.
YOU DO UNDERSTAND *IN YOUR BONES* –
THE LOGISTICS –
THE GENETIC FINAGLING –
THAT WENT INTO *GETTING YOU HERE* –
LONG BEFORE YOUR SOLAR SYSTEM –
OR EVEN *GALAXY* –
WAS EVER CONCEIVED.
YOU QUITE REMEMBER THE:
UNDIFFEENTIATED VOID –
ALWAYS YOUR HOME.
ALWAYS WAS –
ALWAYS WILL BE.
THAT IS NOT IN QUESTION.
……..
When you talk about your GREATER BEING –
You have friends who chide you:

"THIS 3D WORKADAY WORLD IS ENOUGH FOR ME!"

And you feel sorry for them.

You present an analogy.

You say:

"THERE ARE TEN DIMENSIONS I AM ACTIVELY INVOLVED WITH.

THE CORE OF THE EARTH, 1D.

THE TELLURIC REALM, BETWEEN EARTH'S CORE AND CRUST, 2D.

THE SURFACE OF THE EARTH, 3D.

THE INDIVIDUAL AND COLLECTIVE *MENTAL* ATMOSPHERE, 4D.

SAMADHI, THE ONENESS OF ALL LIFE, 5D.

PATTERNS, DESTINIES, DNA, 6D.

THE MUSIC OF THE SPHERES, 7D.

LIGHT, 8D.

THE BLACK HOLE AT THE CENTER OF THE GALAXY, 9D.

AND ALL OF THESE DIMENSIONS *OPERATING AS A WHOLE*, 10D."

You tell them:

"I have ten fingers.

I need all of them –

To grab something.

To play a piano.

HOW SILLY I WOULD LOOK –

SAYING I'M ONLY GOING TO USE ONE OF MY FINGERS!

SAYING YOU ONLY LIVE IN 3D –

AND THAT IS ENOUGH –

IS LIKE TRYING TO PLAY A BEETHOVEN SONATA WITH ONLY ONE FINGER."

You explain to them:

"BEING A CELESTIAL ISN'T *AS OPPOSED TO* BEING A HUMAN."

You say:

"HUMAN IS ONE OF MY FINGERS."

YOU EMPHASIZE:

"THE HUMAN BODY IS REMARKABLY CAPABLE OF HOUSING –

ACCOMODATING –

GROUNDING –

UPLIFTING –

ALL OF THESE DIMENSIONS –

SIMULTANEOUSLY."

YOU ADD:

"THE HUMAN FINGER IS *NOT NOTHING* –

BUT IT IS *NOT EVERYTHING*.

EXCEPT IN THE SENSE THAT ALL DIMENSIONS ARE HOLOGRAMS OF EACH OTHER.

BUT THE CELESTIAL IS A:

COLLECTIVE.

A CONGLOMERATION.

A MACROCOSMIC AND MICROCOSMIC INCLUSIVITY.

THE VERY INTERGALACTIC FEDERATION ITSELF."

That is why you feel sorry for your human friends.

Who still think that they are human.

....

Maybe it is SURVIIVOR'S GUILT.

YOU HAVE SURVIVED THE APOCALYPSE.

MOST OF YOUR HUMAN FRIENDS ARE STILL IN THE MIDST OF IT –

OR HAVEN'T EVEN BEGUN IT YET.

WHO KNEW THE APOCALYPSE WAS THE NECESSARY CATALYST FOR EVOLUTIONARY LEAPFROGGING!

……..

It is a LITTLE BIT LONELY.

Knowing that you do not live in the same world as most of your friends.

(World here is meant in the generic sense of "this place where you are."

It is more MULTIVERSE/OMINVERSE than world.)

But then you smile.

BECAUSE YOU REMEMBER HOW MANY COUNTLESS FRIENDS YOU HAVE IN THE *ENTIRETY* –

OF THIS GARGANTUAN –

MEGALITHIC –

MULTIDMENSIONAL –

INTERGALACTIC –

COMPREHENSIVE --

OCEANIC:

INFINITY –

THAT NOW IS:

THIS PLACE WHERE YOU ARE.

EARTH IS BUT A DROP IN THE BUCKET.

YOU THROW BACK YOUR HEAD AND LAUGH –

WHEN YOU GRASP –

COMPREHEND –

SEE WITH YOUR OWN EYES –

REGISTER WITH YOUR OWN NERVOUS SYSTEM –
THAT YOU HAVE –
IN FACT –
ACHIEVED A:
TRUE –
AND LITERAL:
OMNIPRESENCE.
....
There is who you ARE.
And there is WHAT YOU LOOK LIKE.
When you look into a mirror –
YOU CAN GAZE INTO YOUR OWN EYES –
AND TUMBLE INTO THAT INFINITY.
You can PRIMP.
You can admire your PHYSIQUE –
You can admire your STYLE.
You can find fault –
AND WHAT DO YOU DO WITH THAT?
Do you think there is a CORRELATION –
BETWEEN WHO IS LOOKING AND WHAT YOU ARE LOOKING AT?
YOU CAN LOOK AT THE WORLD MIRROR.
YOUR HOUSE.
YOUR TOWN OR CITY.
YOUR FRIENDS.
YOUR LANDSCAPE, OR SEASCAPE.
YOUR SKIES.
YOUR COUNTRY.
YOUR SOCIETY.

YOUR PLANETARY COLLECTIVE.

YOUR SOLAR SYSTEM.

YOUR GALAXY.

YOUR INTERGALACTIC COLLECTIVE.

THE MICROSCOPIC LIFE TEEMING IN YOUR BODY AND IN YOUR WORLD.

THE MOLECULAR AND SUBATOMIC *LIFE* TEEMING IN YOUR BODY AND IN YOUR WORLD.

And what about your dream life, or places you go in altered states or out of your body?

ARE THESE OTHER WORLDS AS REAL AS YOUR EARTH LIFE?

Of course they are.

YOU CAN SEE HOW *ARBITRARY* IT IS TO THINK IN TERMS OF "INNER" AND "OUTER."

BUT THE QUESTION IS STILL VALID:

WHAT IS THE RELATIONSHIP BETWEEN WHO IS LOOKING AND WHAT IS BEING LOOKED AT?

BUT EVEN THAT TURNS OUT TO BE STRANGELY ARBITRARY.

THE *I AM* IN YOU IS THE SAME *I AM* THAT IS ANIMATING EVERY OTHER PERSON (OR ANIMAL OR TREE OR ROCK OR STAR OR CELL OR ATOM OR QUARK) IN YOUR WORLD OR ANY WORLD YOU FIND YOURSELF IN IN YOUR DREAMS OR OTHERDIMENSIONAL TRAVELS.

YOUR *I AM* PERMEATES EVERY IOTA OF EVERY WORLD YOU ARE *PART OF*.

AND YES THAT IS A BETTER WAY OF SAYING IT.

IT'S NOT LIKE YOU VISIT WORLDS AS A SEPARATE OBJECT, OR EVEN AS AN OBJECTIVE EXPLORER.

WHEN YOU PARTAKE IN A WORLD YOU ARE ALREADY,

BY DEFINITION, THROUGH AND THROUGH, *INFUSED WITHIN IT*.

YOUR EYEBALLS ARE SUDDENLY LOOKING AT YOU FROM EVERY PERSON, CAT, HOUSEFLY, HYBISCUS, CONSTELLATION, ELECTRON.

HONESTLY THE *INTIMACY* IS OVERWHELMING AND SO YOU FIND WAYS TO "MITIGATE" IT.

DENY IT.

REPRESS IT.

EXPLAIN IT AWAY.

RAGE AGAINST IT.

JUDGE IT.

CONDEMN IT.

ARGUE WITH IT.

TRY TO KILL IT.

A BETTER WAY OF SAYING IT?

THE LOVE IS OVERWHELMING.

....

Yes.

YOU ARE GOING TO HAVE TO GROW INTO THIS.

THAT'S OK.

YOU HAVE LEARNED:

THAT NO MATTER WHAT:

NO MATTER HOW EGREGIOUS YOUR BEHAVIOR –

OR ANYONE ELSE'S –

THE PROPER RESPONSE –

THE MATURE RESPONSE –

THE *ENLIGHTENED* RESPONSE –

IS:

"IT'S OK. IT'S OK. IT'S OK."

YOUR HEART IS OPEN NOW THE BREADTH OF EXPONENTIALY IMPOSSIBLE MULTIVERSES.

THAT IS SIMPLY AN *ANATOMICAL FEATURE* –

OF THE NEW SPECIES THAT YOU ARE.

In short:

YOU ARE A BETTER PERSON THAN YOU THINK YOU ARE.

YOU REALLY CAN'T HELP IT.

....

You will need a break.

FROM THIS MULTIDIMENSIONAL ONSLAUGHT OF LOVE.

Well, it's not exactly a BREAK.

BUT IT WILL FEEL LIKE ONE.

LET'S SAY THERE IS A –

BUILT-IN –

HELPER.

IT'S ANOTHER PART OF YOUR ANATOMY NOW.

Here's how it works:

THE NEXT SPECIES YOU ARE EVOLVING INTO –

(AND YOU KNOW BY NOW –

THE UNIVERSE IS ORGANIZED BY THESE:

EVOLUTIONARY ECHELONS) –

THE NEXT SPECIES YOU ARE EVOLVING INTO:

IS ALREADY –

ALSO:

PART OF YOUR ANATOMY.

THE "GUARDIAN ANGEL" IS BUILT IN.

AND IT IS *NOT* FAR AWAY.

IT IS NOT INACCESSIBLE.

IN FACT:

IT IS NEARLY AS ACCESSIBLE AS THE SELF YOU IDENTIFY WITH.

THE FACT IS:

IT IS ALWAYS THERE.

ALWAYS WHISPERING.

SMILING.

SWEET-TALKING YOU –

LAUGHING NOT AT YOU BUT WITH YOU –

ALL THE *SHARED VICISSITUDES.*

THIS FUTURE SELF IS NOT HAUGHTY –

OR SUPERIOR.

IT IS A FRIEND.

IT IS YOUR BEST FRIEND.

....

IT WILL TELL YOU –

GUIDE YOU –

ADVISE YOU:

"YOU NEED REST.

SLEEP.

LIE DOWN.

THERE IS NO SUCH THING AS TOO MUCH REST AND SLEEP.

AND MEDITATION?

FORGET ABOUT MEDITATION.

EVERYTHING YOU THOUGHT WAS MEDITATION IS A SCAM –

A SCAM DESIGNED BY VERY UNKIND –

ACTUALLY:

UNENLIGHTENED –

PEOPLE –

WHO DID NOT KNOW HOW TO LOVE THEMSELVES –

OR ANYONE ELSE.

THEY CERTAINLY DO NOT LOVE YOU.

BUT I DO.

THEY DO NOT KNOW ANYTHING ABOUT MEDITATION.

BUT I DO.

DON'T SIT.

LIE DOWN.

CLOSE YOUR EYES.

FEEL THE THROB OF WHO YOU ARE.

WHEN YOU GO DEEPLY INTO YOURSELF YOU WILL NOT FIND SILENCE.

YOU WILL FIND *THROBBING*.

YOU WILL FIND YOUR HEARTBEAT.

YOU WILL FEEL THE BLOOD *PULSING* THROUGH EVERY DELICIOUS, SAVORY MORSEL OF YOUR GLORIOUS MAGNIFICENT BODY.

LISTEN.

IT IS NOT ONLY THE STARS THAT SING THE MUSIC OF THE SPHERES!

IF YOU *LISTEN:*

YOU WILL HEAR EVERY CELL AND EVERY ATOM OF YOUR BODY SINGING –

BELLOWING –

THE HALLAJUAH CHORUS!

AND IF YOU FALL ASLEEP –

THAT IS WONDERFUL!

TAKE YOUR MEDITATION INTO SLEEP.

ANY YOGI –

ANY SAINT –

WORTH HIS SALT –

WILL TELL YOU THAT:

SLEEP IS THE BEST MEDITATION OF ALL.

YOU MIGHT START OUT MEDITATING:

TEN MINUTES.

ONCE THAT IS COMFORTABLE –

GO TO AN HOUR.

THEN THREE HOURS.

THEN TWELVE.

ONCE YOU UNDERSTAND THAT THIS *MEDITATION THAT IS NOT A MEDITATION* IS NOT SOMETHING YOU ARE DOING –

BUT RATHER:

IT IS SOMETHING THAT IS *BEING DONE TO YOU* –

THEN YOU WILL KNOW –

AND YOU AND I WILL BOTH LAUGH –

WHEN YOU REALIZE –

RECEIVE THE *SHAKTIPAT* –

THAT THIS *MEDITATION THAT IS NOT A MEDITATION* –

IS:

ALSO:

A FEATURE OF YOUR NEW ANATOMY.

IT IS WHO YOU ARE.

YOU COULDN'T STOP IT IF YOU TRIED.

SO THIS:

MEDITATION THAT IS NOT A MEDITATION –

THIS REST –

THIS *HAVEN* –

THIS OASIS –

THIS *HEAVEN* –

IS WHO YOU ARE.

IT IS CONTINUOUS.

IT IS SEAMLESS.

TWENTY-FOUR HOURS A DAY.

OR WHATEVER TIME MEASUREMENT YOUR ASTRONOMICAL SYSTEM EMPLOYS."

....

You may not know exactly why you are here.

BUT YOU KNOW THAT THERE IS A PART OF YOU THAT DOES.

All the WHYS and WHEREFORES.

And the WHENCES.

And HENCES.

And all the NUANCES.

You have been told:

OMNISCIENCE IS SIMPLY A PERMANENT STATE OF ASTONISHMENT.

So you suppose that you –

ABSOLUTELY ARE.

At least enough to SATISFY.

You notice:

YOU REALLY *DON'T* HAVE ANY BURNING

QUESTIONS.
LIFE IS SWEET.
YOU FEEL LIKE YOU JUST GOT MARRIED.
YOUR *NEW FRIEND* IS ABSOLUTELY THE MOST:
ATTENTIVE LOVER YOU HAVE EVER HAD.
In fact:
You suspect:
THAT EVERY LOVER YOU EVER HAD WAS A –
PEEK –
A:
TEMPORARY INCARNATION –
OF THIS FUTURE SELF –
WHO HAS BEEN LURING YOU –
TEASING YOU –
FLIRTING WITH YOU –
EVER SINCE --
BEFORE YOU EVEN WERE BORN.
You want to call this new LOVER:
Your SELF.
BECAUSE YOU KNOW THAT THEY *ARE*.
BUT OUT OF:
DEFERENCE –
REVERENCE –
HUMILITY –
AND PERHAPS MOST OF ALL –
OUT OF:
LONGING –
YOU FIND IT –

SEEMLY –

PROPER –

THEMATICALLY *APPEALING* –

TO HAVE JUST THE HAIR'S BREADTH –

OF A DISTINCTION BETWEEN YOU.

YOU KNOW THAT HE/SHE/IT LOOKS OUT OF YOUR EYES.

AND YOU *LIKE* THAT!

BUT –

CALL IT A:

WHIMSICAL –

WISHFUL –

ROMANITC –

LOVER'S *PREROGATIVE.*

YOU WANT –

YOU *LONG* –

TO GAZE INTO –

TO FALL INTO –

GET LOST IN:

THOSE *STRANGE* –

NOT TERRIFYING –

BUT MYSTERIOUS –

NUMINOUS:

EYES.

……..

AND YOU FIND THAT THIS LOVER IS *ALL TOO EAGER* TO COMPLY.

YOU KNOW VERY WELL THAT HE/SHE/IT *SET UP SHOP* –

ESTABLISHED DOMICILE –
IN EVERY LOVER YOU'VE EVER HAD.
MAYBE FOR YEARS.
MAYBE FOR ONLY A MOMENT.
YOU SUSPECT A PET OR TWO –
ALSO HOUSED THIS MAGNIFICENCE –
IF ONLY FOR THE LIFETIME THAT WAS ALLOWED.
(THOUGH OF COURSE YOU STILL HAVE DREAMS.
JUMPING UP ON YOU –
LICKING –
TAIL WAGGING.
OR HEAD NUZZLING –
AUDIBLE PURRING.)
THIS NEW:
MAGNIFICENT FRIENDSHIP –
ISN'T EXACTLY SEXUAL.
IT ISN'T –
NOT –
SEXUAL.
THE CIRCUITRY IS THERE.
AND THE:
CHEMISTRY.
THE ELECTRICITY.
THE:
THRILL.
BUT THE FACT IS:
YOUR SEXUAL NEEDS –
FANTASIES –

FETISHES –
REQUIREMENTS –
WERE SATISFIED –
AND I MEAN:
SATIATED –
I MEAN:
QUENCHED –
LONG AGO.
THE ONLY REMAINING *ECHO* OF THOSE –
HAPPY –
WILD –
LURID –
DOMESTIC –
ADVENTUROUS –
EXPLOSIVE –
HISTORICAL –
NEARLY MYTHICAL:
ENTANGLEMENTS –
IS THE SWEETEST –
SMUGGEST –
BARELY PERCEPTIBLE:
AMPLY SATISFIED:
SMILE –
THAT LIINGERS ON YOUR LIPS –
AND ALWAYS WILL.
……..
THAT WAS DONE.
AND IT WAS DONE WELL.

IT WAS DONE:
THOROUGHLY.
EVERY ROMANTIC FANTASY –
EVERY EROTIC:
KINK –
WAS SATISFIED –
UTTERLY –
AND MANY TIMES OVER –
TO COMPLETION.
TO:
FINALIZATION.
YOU SUSPECT THAT –
FROM OUTER SPACE –
YOUR *AFTERGLOW* –
RESEMBLES A:
SUPERNOVA –
GUIDING GENERATIONS OF LOVERS –
ON THEIR WINDING –
AGONIZING –
ROLLERCOASTER –
EPIC –
TRAGIC –
TRIUMPANT –
ACCOMPLISHMENT –
ACHIEVEMENT –
FULFILLMENT –
COMPLETION –
AND *FINALLY:*

GRADUATION.

....

SEEING THEIR:

SAGA –

YOU GRASP –

A PRODUCT OF YOUR NEWFOUND OMNISCIENCE –

THAT WHAT YOU HAVE –

ACTUALLY –

GRADUATED FROM:

IS:

HUMANITY.

PART FOUR

Remember:

WE ARE LYING DREAMILY IN BED.

You know that SCHOOL will be starting soon.

So you LUXURIATE in this most

DELICOUS of INDULGES.

You find yourself:

DREADING –

Having to set your alarm clock –

Bracing for the COLD outside this COCOON –

This NEST.

This WOMB.

But then –

IN A SHOW OF:

INTENTIONAL GLEE AT GIFTING YOU WITH A SURPISE THAT I KNOW WILL PUT A SMILE ON THOSE SWEET LIPS –

I AM THERE –

WHISPERING IN YOUR EAR:

"No.

You are already in your CLASSROOM.

Keep the covers pulled up around your chin.

Yawn and stretch a bit –

BECAUSE WE ARE GETTING READY TO BEGIN."

....

I tell you:

"The only TEXTBOOK you will need is:

YOUR OWN BODY."

I continue:

"THAT'S THE REASON IT WAS GIVEN TO YOU IN THE FIRST PLACE."

The responding facial expression of SLEEPY DELIGHT –

Is honestly WHAT I WAKE UP FOR EVERY MORNING.

MAKES IT ALL WORTH IT.

I *PUZZLE YOU FURTHER* by explaining:

"I WILL BE GIVING YOU A GUIDED TOUR OF YOUR OWN BODY."

Your COMPREHENSION is *INSTANTANEOUS.*

In fact:

IT APPEARS AS THOUGH YOU HEAR ME EVEN BEFORE THE WORDS HAVE LEFT MY LIPS.

I look BESEECHINGLY INTO YOUR EYES –

As you look:

BESEECHINGLY INTO MY OWN EYES –

In a SIMULTANEOUS *SHARED KNOWING SHOCK.*

You realize –

INSTANTAINOUS WITH MY OWN REALIZATON –

That:

YOU:

ALMOST CAN'T NOT:

NOT DISTINGUISH --

BETWEEN THE TWO OF US.

The jig is up.

The JOKE is up.

AND YET WE BOTH LAUGH.

Clearly –

THIS *FALSE FLAG* –
IS A GAME –
WE BOTH WANT TO CONTINUE PLAYING.
....
This curriculum is NOT SCRIPTED.
Honestly –
When I saw that you –
HEARD MY WORDS –
BEFORE I'D SAID THEM –
OR EVEN *THOUGHT* THEM –
I was momentarily –
TAKEN ABACK.
As if there had almost been a:
SECURITY BREACH.
My OWN *INSECURITY* –
VULNERABILITY –
Was a SURPRISE –
Not only to you –
But to myself.
EVEN WHEN IT COMES TO SPECIES –
THE TEACHER –
THE *EVOLUTIONARY PROGENY* –
IS ONLY A STEP OR TWO BEYOND THE STUDENT.
IT IS NO WONDER THAT YOU SOMETIMES CAN'T QUITE –
TELL THE DIFFERENCE BETWEEN US.
BETWEEN MY SHOCK AND YOURS.
....
And yet that awareness in itself –

Is an evolutionary STRETCH.

LEAP even.

The realization that:

I DON'T KNOW WHERE THIS IS GOING –

ANY MORE THAN YOU DO –

IS IN ITSELF –

AN ENTIRE BLOCK OF INFORMATION –

PERHAPS EVEN *LIBRARY BRACH* –

OF THE AKASHIC RECORDS.

LIKE YOU COULD GET AN ENTIRE PH.D. ON THE SUBJECT.

FINDING MYSELF AT A LOSS –

I LOOK FORWARD –

LOOK AHEAD –

TO MY OWN:

FUTURE SELF.

AND NOW I SEE HIM/SHE/IT –

IN AN ALTOGETHER NEW –

AND SYMPATHETIC LIGHT.

WHAT A *STUNNER* –

TO BOTH OF US –

THAT:

I DON'T KNOW WHERE THIS IS GOING ANY MORE THAN YOU DO.

AN EVEN BIGGER:

PUNCH IN THE GUT –

IS GUESSING –

DEDUCING –

THAT MY OWN:

FUTURE SELF –
IS:
JUST AS MUCH AT A LOSS.
....
And then I remember the lesson –
The DEFINITION –
You and I have both –
Only recently received:
OMNISCIENCE SIMPLY MEANS:
BEING IN A CONTINUOUS STATE OF:
ASTONISHMENT.
In which case:
YOU –
ME –
AND MY OWN FUTURE SELF –
ARE MORE:
ADVANCED –
THAN WE KNEW.
....
Randy just spent four hours in DEEP MEDITATION –
Saying the HO'OPONOPONO phrases.
We told him:
"THAT WAS GLORIOUS.
We're SO GLAD we titled our last book:
GLORIOUS.
That is an ACCURATE DESCRIPTION –
Of what WE –
And YOU –

DO.”
THERE ARE MANY WAYS TO *COME AT* THE:
EVOLUTIONARY REQUIREMENT –
Of GETTING NOT JUST THE EGO –
BUT THE *CONSCIOUS MIND* –
OUT OF THE WAY –
OR AT LEAST OF:
MAKING IT *TRANSPARENT* –
SO THAT THE:
EPSILON –
OF THE ENTIRE *SPECTRUM* –
OF YOUR *FUTURE SELVES* –
YOU –
AT THE *HIGHER ECHELONS* OF YOUR SELF –
UP TO AND INCLUDING:
THE GODHEAD –
THE VOID –
THE GREAT I AM –
Can *SHINE THROUGH.*
And I’ll briefly define:
THE EPSILON –
Again here.
Let’s say you are the number:
MINUS ONE.
And you’ve got your eye on becoming:
ZERO.
You will have to:
INCH YOUR WAY UP,

You see.
You'll start by HALVING the distance.
So now you are MINUS ONE HALF.
THAT'S QUITE AN ACCOMPLISHMENT!
So you decide to HALF THE DISTANCE AGAIN.
And now you are MINUS ONE QUARTER.
The process –
YOUR GROWTH –
IS *SO SATISFYING* –
That you actually –
DON'T MIND THE --
ETERNITY –
IT WILL TAKE TO GET TO YOUR DESTINATION.
As things progress –
EITHER AT YOUR PACE –
OR MORE LIKELY –
AT *LIFE'S* PACE –
You pass by:
MILESTONE AFTER MILESTONE.
MINUS ONE FIFTIETH.
MINUS ONE HUNDREDTH.
(We're talking *EONS* here!)
MINUS ONE THOUSANDTH.
MINUS ONE MILLIONTH.
MINUS ONE BILLIONTH.
At some point –
The HORROR will dawn upon you –
That you will NEVER ACTUALLY GET THERE!

NEVER!
EVER!
EVER!
……..
This does present an:
EXISTENTIAL CRISIS –
Of INCALCULABLE –
DEVASTATING –
MAGNITUDE.
UNTIL YOU HEAR:
MY –
WHISPER:
"DARLING…
DON'T YOU SEE?
YOU WERE THERE –
HERE --
ALL ALONG.
ZERO –
THE VOID –
GODHEAD –
THE GREAT *I AM* –
THIS IS WHO YOU:
ALREADY ARE.
ALWAYS HAVE BEEN.
ALWAYS WILL BE.
COULDN'T:
NOT:
BE.

....

I continue –
AS I WRESTLE YOU TO THE GROUND –
AND TICKLE YOUR RIBS –
NOW *THAT'S* THE HAPPY FACE I LIKE TO SEE!
"TECHNICALLY –
THIS JOURNEY –
THIS QUEST –
THIS PILGRIM'S PROGRESS –
THIS *CREAKING* –
GLACIAL –
EVOLUTIONARY –
FRACTALING UNFOLDMENT:
FROM THE HYPOTHETICAL:
BIG BANG –
TO:
YOU –
IS UTTERLY –
CATEGORICALLY –
INCONTROVERTIBLY ---
UNNECESSARY.
YOU –
AND I DO MEAN:
YOU:
WERE THE *DESTINATION* –
ALL ALONG.
YOU AS:
GODHEAD.

YOU AS:
ZERO.
YOU AS:
THE VOID.
YOU:
AS:
THE GREAT I AM.
WHICH IS:
UTTERLY –
CATEGORICALLY –
INCONTROVERTIBLY –
WHO YOU:
ARE:
AND WERE:
ALWAYS WILL BE:
COULDN'T –
NOT BE:
IF YOU TRIED.
……..
So WHAT WAS IT ALL FOR?
Well –
I'll tell you.
THE REASON FOR –
IT ALL –
IS:
THIS:
VERY --
KNOWLEDGE –

INSIGHT –
SHAKTIPAT.
Let's face it:
YOU DIDN'T KNOW THIS BEFORE.
THROUGH ALL THAT:
DRUDGING –
SCROUNGING –
MEANDERING –
THROUGH THE DESERT –
THE FOREST –
OUTER SPACE –
YOU HAD NO IDEA –
THAT THE:
DESTINATION:
WAS:
YOU.
AND *NOW YOU DO.*
....
The ECHELONS are still there.
The EPSILON continues spinning its:
NEVER CEASING VORTEX.
YOU NOW –
IMAGINE:
THE CIVILIZATIONS –
WHO MUST DWELL –
AT THE MILESTONE:
NEGATIVE ONE GOOGOL-TH.
(A googol is the number one followed by 100 zeros.)

Those folks must be PRETTY FUCKING DARNED COOL!
Maybe you do a little house hunting there.
To settle down.
For awhile.
YOU WONDER IF THEY KNOW –
AS YOU DO NOW:
THAT YOU ARE ALL:
ALREADY THERE.

PART FIVE

Our EXPERIMENT is MULTI-PRONGED –

And MULTI-LAYERED.

The CALCULATIONS that went into it would be INCOMPREHENSIBLE to you –

But NOT REALLY.

Not in any ABSOLUTE terms.

YOU WOULD HAVE TO:

BECOME US –

IN ORDER TO:

UNDERSTAND US.

But you should know by now –

THAT ISN'T THE *HOODINI FEAT* –

You used to think it was.

You know now that:

ANY FLEA OR AMOEBA IS IN FACT –

NO OTHER THAN –

NO LESS THAN –

AND *NOTHING BUT* –

THE INTERGALACTIC FEDERATION –

IN ITS ENTIRETY.

The EVOLUTIONARY WORK –

Is not in *BECOMING* ALL OF THIS –

BECAUSE:

YOU ALREADY ARE.

The evolutionary *TRIUMPH* –

Is simply in the AWARENESS.

The KNOWLEDGE.

Of course –

(AND THIS IS NOT A *MINOR POINT* –

THOUGH I WILL INSIST IT IS INCIDENTAL –

IF ONLY IN THE SENSE THAT THE RESULTS ARE SPONTANEOUS –

AND DO QUITE TAKE CARE OF THEMSELVES) –

AS ONE'S AWARENESS –

AS ONE'S *KNOWLEDGE* –

EVOLVES –

THEN SO TOO –

A NEW:

BODY –

WILL BE REQUIRED.

YOU CAN'T CHANGE:

WHO YOU ARE –

WITHOUT CHANGING:

WHAT YOU LOOK LIKE.

As well as your:

ANATOMICAL FUNCTIONALITY.

You will have:

EXTRA ARMS.

OR THEY WILL BEND IN A NEW WAY.

PERHAPS LIKE AN INSECT.

OR YOU WILL HAVE *EXTRA HEARTS.*

AND MANY OF THESE HEARTS WILL BE:

OUTSIDE YOUR OBVIOUS –

SO-CALLED:

BODY.

You see:

YOU MAY FIND THAT YOUR BODY IS:

OUTSIDE OF YOU.

You may VERY WELL discover –

That your WORLD –

AND WHO IS TO SAY THAT THERE IS ONLY *ONE* WORLD?

YOU MOST CERTAINLY WILL FIND THAT YOU HAVE *JUST AS MANY WORLDS* –

AS YOU HAVE *HEARTS.*

But yes you may very well find:

That your WORLD –

IN FACT, YOUR *WORLDS* –

ARE NOW A KIND OF:

SECONDARY BODY.

AND YES YOU MAY VERY WELL FIND THAT YOU HAVE MULTIPLE SECONDARY BODIES.

But you won't worry about it.

It really does TAKE CARE OF ITSELF.

There may be a brief *TRANSITIONAL PERIOD* –

Where you ENJOY –

LIKE A BABY –

EXPLORING YOUR NEW:

RANGES OF MOBILITY AND FUNCTIONALITY.

Fortunately –

FOR EVERYONE! –

You have –

FINALLY –

GRASPED –

INTERNALIZED –

BY *EXPERIENCE* –

That NO ONE IS OUT TO GET YOU.

But quite the contrary.

....

Our GUINEA PIG Randy –

Is a treasure.

A PRIZE –

EVEN TO HIMSELF.

Don't worry.

There is no DISSECTION.

Better yet:

There is no *VIVISECTION*.

There are no CHEMICAL TESTS –

ALTHOUGH THERE WAS SOME EXTREMELY PRODUCTIVE EXPERIMENTATION WITH:

ALCOHOL –

CRYSTAL METH –

AYAHUASCA.

There were no STRESS TESTS, exactly.

And yet:

THERE WAS A FAMILY WHERE PHYSICAL VIOLENCE WAS A DAILY OCCURANCE.

THERE WERE BULLIES IN SCHOOL.

THERE WERE MULTIPLE LIFE-THREATENING ILLNESSES.

THERE WAS ONE SEVEN MONTH PERIOD OF SLEEPING ON COLD SIDEWALKS.

THERE WAS THE:

ENDURING –

OF WATCHING HIS:
EXTERNAL WORLD –
DIE:
ONE SPARROW –
ONE POLAR BEAR –
ONE RIVER –
AT A TIME.
DEATH BY A THOUSAND CUTS.
NO LESS –
GRISLY –
AGONIZING –
THAN THAT *SLOW METHOD OF EXECUTION* –
FROM IMPERIAL CHINA.
ALMOST:
THE *GIFT:*
OF:
SAVORING:
DEATH.
....
If worlds are SCHOOLS –
AND THEY ARE –
Then YOU COULD SAY:
THAT RANDY HAS A PH.D. IN:
DEATH.
YOU WOULD BE HARD-PRESSED TO FIND A MORE CHALLENGING –
AND REWARDING –
SUBJECT.
....

A couple of days ago –
Randy was meditating.
He was in his fourth hour.
His eyes were closed.
He CAUGHT HIMSELF DOING SOMETHING.
IT TOOK HIM AWHILE TO FIGURE OUT WHAT WAS GOING ON.
EVEN THOUGH HIS EYES WERE CLOSED –
HE WAS *LOOKING AROUND THE ROOM* –
AND SEEING EVERYTHING WITH PERFECT CLARITY.
LESSON:
BODIES –
ARE NOT LIMITED –
TO ONE DIMENSION –
ONLY.
THEY NEVER HAVE BEEN.
BUT THEY SURE AS FUCK ARE NOT –
NOW.
EVEN WRITING ABOUT IT NOW:
RANDY LAUGHS.
ONE:
TRICK:
THAT YOU LEARN:
WHEN YOU OPEN UP TO THE:
FACT:
OF MULTIPLE DIMENSIONS –
IS THAT:
SUDDENLY –

YOU *REALIZE* –
YOU KNOW –
THAT:
THE WORLD IS NOT A PRISON.
NO WORLD –
NO DIMENSION –
IS A PRISON.
BASICALLY:
YOU COME AND GO AS YOU PLEASE.
ANOTHER:
TRICK:
THAT YOU WILL LEARN –
AND NOT JUST BY KNOWLEDGE BUT BY:
DIRECT EXPERIENCE --
IS THAT:
ALL WORLDS –
ALL DIMENSIONS:
ARE INHERENTLY:
DELICIOUS.
AND DELIGHTFUL.
AND *MULTIFARIOUSLY SO.*
BECAUSE YOU:
HAVE:
IRREFUTABLY:
BECOME:
DELICIOUS –
DELIGHTFUL --
AND *MULTIFARIOUS* –

YOURSELF.

....

AS BELOW –
SO ABOVE.
THE WORLD –
ANY WORLD –
ALL WORLDS –
SHOW YOU WHO YOU ARE.
AND:
VICE VERSA.
AND THAT IS ONE HELL OF A:
TRICK:
TO IMPRESS YOUR FRIENDS WITH:
AT DINNER PARTIES.

....

This afternoon Randy meditated for four hours.
There was no HO'OPONOPONO.
There was no SAYING ANYTHING.
UNTIL THERE WAS.
For the last several days we have been telling him to:
FIND YOU HEARTBEAT.
FIND YOUR:
FULL BODY THROB.
So he was PREPARED.
TODAY:
HE WENT INSIDE HIS OPEN HEART.
AND IT WAS WONDERFUL.
HE KNOWS THAT IS WHERE:

EVERYTHING IS.
ONCE YOUR HEART OPENS –
ALL SPIRITUAL TECHNIQUES –
PRACTICES –
FALL AWAY –
OR RATHER:
GET:
DEVOURED.
CONSUMED.
SUBSUMED.
EVEN HO'OPONOPONO.
We told him yesterday:
"THE ONLY THING MORE EFFECTIVE THAN HO'OPONOPONO IS:
SILENCE."
OF COURSE WHAT WE MEANT WAS:
THE *OPEN HEART*.
THE VOID.
THE GODHEAD.
ALL THAT IS.
WHO YOU REALLY ARE.
WHO EVERYONE AND EVERYTHING REALLY IS.
THERE ARE *DESIRES* THAT:
BUBBLE UP:
FROM THIS OPEN HEART.
THESE DESIRES ARE NOT EGOIC.
THEY ARE NOT:
INTENTIONAL.
THEY WILL ALWAYS BE A SURPRISE.

THEY ARE INSPIRATION.

THEY ARE DIVINE.

Well…

THREE DESIRES DID BUBBLE UP FOR RANDY TODAY.

WE HAVE BEEN WEANING HIM OFF MANIFESTATION TECHNIQUES.

Basically we told him:

"THAT'S NO FUN.

NOT FOR ANYONE.

ESPECIALLY NOT FOR *US.*"

We told him:

"IF YOU WANT SOMETHING –

IF YOU HAVE A DESIRE –

BUBBLING –

ASK US TO GIVE IT TO YOU."

Many years ago Randy got an unusually expensive electric bill.

He couldn't pay it.

He mentioned this to his therapist Sue and she told him:

"DO YOUR PARENTS A FAVOR AND ASK THEM FOR THE MONEY."

He did.

AND THE SHARED JOY WAS PALPABLE.

So…

OBEDIENTLY:

RANDY ASKED US TO GIVE HIM THESE THREE THINGS.

OUR –

PALPABLY –

JOYOUS –
RESPONSE WAS:
"DONE.
AND DONE.
AND DONE."
In the last half hour –
SWIMMING –
DROWNING –
IN AN OCEAN OF LOVE –
AN OCEAN OF *OUR* LOVE –
OURS AND RANDY'S –
RECIPROCAL–
LOVE –
WE:
COMMENTED:
"THIS FEELS LIKE BEING MARRIED, DOESN'T IT?"
YOU SHOULD HAVE SEEN THE SWEET SWEET CURL OF RANDY'S LIPS –
WHEN HE SAID –
SIMPLY –
"YEAH."

PART SIX

The biggest change you will notice is that:

EVERYTHING IS INFUSED WITH LIGHT.

But let me be careful how I explain that.

Light isn't "ADDED."

It isn't "BROUGHT IN" from the:

HIGHER DIMENSIONS.

The DIMENSIONS are *INTERWOVEN* –

In a way that is MOST WONDROUS.

There is no *SPACIAL SEPARATION* of the dimensions.

They are not in DIFFERENT LOCATIONS.

They are *ALL HERE NOW*.

In fact, HERE AND NOW IS THE ONLY "PLACE" THERE EVER IS –

OR EVER *CAN* BE.

That in itself will REVOLUTIONIZE your understanding of:

TRAVEL.

Including *SPACE TRAVEL.*

It will also TOPPLE and TURN UPSIDE DOWN –

Your notions of EVOLUTION –

Or SPIRITUAL GROWTH.

RIGHT HERE RIGHT NOW –

Is SYNONYMOUS with:

ALL THAT IS.

This would include:

EVEN THE MOST BIZZARE OF ALTERNATE –

ANTI-MATER –

BLACK HOLE –

BACKWARDS TIME –

NO TIME –

LAND OF THE GIANTS –

CIVILIZATIONS OF QUARKS –

FAR BEYOND SYMBOLS OR EVEN *THOUGHTS* –

REALITIES.

We have referred to the SELF as:

GRAND CENTRAL STATION OF THE INTERGALACTIC FEDERATION –

And that is what:

EVERY ATOM –

OR EVERY CELL –

OF *YOU:*

IS.

....

But OH YES THE LIGHT!

IT IS WONDROUS BEYOND DESCRIPTION.

IT BOILS.

IT EXPLODES.

IT INCINERATES.

IT *SINGS.*

For yes:

THIS *LIGHT* IS ALWAYS ACCOMPANIED BY:

MUSIC.

They are a pair, they are!

NEVER ONE WITHOUT THE OTHER.

Of course LIGHT –

Is the EIGHTH DIMENSION.

And SOUND –

The SEVENTH.

It should be stated here:

THERE IS NOTHING THAT THE COMBINATION OF LIGHT AND SOUND CANNOT HEAL –

ACCOMPLISH –

RESOLVE –

MAKE RIGHT.

Together they create the:

PERFECT –

LIGHTNING STORM.

You see:

This LIGHT and SOUND are not:

ADDED,

They are:

UNLEASHED.

....

You are SO AWARE NOW –

That you are at SOMEWHERE AROUND THE:

FIVE TRILLIONTH MILESTONE.

YOU HAVE COME FAR.

YOU ARE NOW A SPECIES THAT ISN'T EVEN:

PERCEPTIBLE –

TO:

*99.999999999999999999999999999999999999999999999
99999999999999999999999999999999999999999999999
99999999999999999999999999999999999999999999999
99999999999999999999999999999999999999999999999
99999999999999999999999999999999999%* --

OF ALL KNOWN SPECIES.

For THEM –

You dwell in the realm of MYTH.

ANCIENT LEGENDS –

DRUM BEATS –

COURSING –

SURGING –

COERCING ITSELF THROUGH THEIR *UNCOMPREHENDING VEINS.*

BUT MAKING ITSELF KNOWN –

FELT –

IN BOTH WORSHIP AND FEAR –

IF ONLY UNCONSCIOUSLY.

Because AT THIS POINT –

You must admit:

For this LARGE SWATH –

OF BEINGS –

CIVILIZATIONS –

You are DWELLING –

Your HOME BASE –

Is the REALM OF THE:

UNCONSCIOUS.

You FEEL THAT POWER.

THE POWER THAT YOU NOW *WEILD*.

THE FACT THAT –

THEY CANNOT SEE YOU –

RENDERS YOU:

BY DEFINITION:

TERRIFYING.

……..

And then you TURN AROUND –
And look in the *OTHER* DIRECTION.
With SHOCK AND:
WONDROUS HUMILITY –
YOU BEGIN TO GRASP –
THAT FOR ANOTHER:
99.9999999999999999999999999999999999999999999999
999999999999999999999999999999999999999999999999
999999999999999999999999999999999999999999999999
999999999999999999999999999999999999999999999999
99999999999999999999999999999999999% --
You are a:
PIP.
A HATCHLING.
JUST NOW SLITHERING OUT OF THE PRIMORDIAL OOZE.
LOOKED UPON WITH:
PITY –
IF AT ALL.
The same way that you might consider:
PROTOZOA.
……..
Do you see –
COMPREHEND –
The BALANCE you have now:
ACCOMPLISHED –
SECURED –
ATTAINED?
For half of ALL BEINGS –
(As if INFINITY can be:

HALVED!) –
You are a GOD.
For the OTHER HALF –
YOU ARE A NEMATODE.
Yes.
It does –
FINALLY –
FEEL –
Like you have found your:
RIGHT PLACE –
IN THE:
SCHEME OF THINGS.
……..
What does this have to do with LIGHT and SOUND?
Of course:
THE SEVENTH AND EIGHTH DIMENSIONS ARE:
POPULATED.
You will have to TOSS OUT –
Most of DARWIN –
FOR THE SIMPLE REASON THAT:
THIS ARRAY –
OF SPECIES –
SPANS:
INTERDIMENSIONAL MULTIVERSES.
Being situated –
As you ARE –
At the (THEORETICAL) –
HALFWAY POINT –

OF THIS:
EVOLUTIONARY PROCESSION –
You GRASP –
ACCURATELY –
That:
YOU HAVE A JOB TO DO.
You have your TOE –
IN A LOT OF *PONDS.*
And therefore:
YOU HAVE GIFTS –
THAT ONLY *YOU* –
CAN GIVE.
....
Do you know how you PROFFER –
These GIFTS?
You quickly realize –
That the GIFT that is most *RECOGNIZED* –
And IN DEMAND –
Is the:
HEALING QUALITY OF THE:
LIGHT AND SOUND –
THAT YOU DO:
BASK –
AND *THRIVE IN* –
CONTINUOUISLY.
You are regarded as a:
MIRACLE WORKER –
AND RIGHTLY SO.

It is WIDELY RECOGNIZED –
WITH AN UNCOMFORTABLE MIXTURE OF:
WONDER –
AND CONSTERNATION –
THAT THIS *IMPOSSIBLE FEAT* –
IS:
FOR YOU:
THE MOST:
OBVIOUS –
AND:
EASY:
THING IN THE WORLD.
You SILENTLY:
And AUTHORITATIVELY:
REASSURE –
Your *BENEFICIARIES* –
Not only of your POWERS –
But your ABILITY to:
BESTOW THEM.
....
How you ARRANGE –
To ACCOMPLISH this –
Is *IN ITSELF* –
NOTHING SHORT OF A MIRACLE.
Or will certainly be:
REGARDED AS SUCH.
Your POSITION –
At the HALFWAY MARK –

In the EVOLUTIONARY PROCESSION –
Does render you:
SUPERNATURALLY RELATABLE.
And this is NOT –
Merely a NICETY.
For you see:
HOW YOU BESTOW –
YOUR GIFT TO THE:
MASSES TO THE LEFT OF YOU –
AND NO LESS –
TO THE MASSES TO THE RIGHT OF YOU:
IS THAT YOU SIMPLY –
AND YES IT IS QUITE EASY FOR YOU AT THIS POINT –
YOU SIMPLY:
UNLEASH –
THE *LIGHT* –
AND THE *SYMPHONIES* –
IN EACH AND EVERY:
CELL –
AND ATOM –
IN YOUR –
OWN:
BODY.
....
NOT ONLY:
OMNISCIENCE –
BUT:
OMNIPRESENCE –

ARE TRAITS –

YOU:

ACQUIRED –

LONG AGO.

You see:

THERE IS NO –

ACTUAL –

BESTOWING.

THERE IS NO:

PROFFERING.

THERE IS NO:

HANDING OUT.

THERE IS NOTHING THAT WOULD *RESEMBLE* ANYTHING THE BARBARIAN RACES ONCE CONCEPTUALIZED AS "GENEROSITY."

IF I –

OR YOU –

WANT TO:

UNLEASH:

LIGHT –

AND:

SYMPHONIC SCREAMING –

IN ANOTHER –

OR A RACE –

OR A WORLD --

ALL I –

OR YOU –

HAVE TO DO –

IS:

UNLEASH –
THIS *FURY* –
OF LIGHT AND SOUND –
IN EVERY:
CELL –
AND ATOM –
IN MY OWN –
OR YOUR OWN –
BODY.
AND THEN:
WATCH –
THE UNLEASHING –
OF HOLY LIGHT –
AND HOLY SOUND –
CASCADE ACROSS THE GLOBE –
ACROSS THE *KALEIDOSCOPE* –
OF DIMENSIONAL INFINITIES –
LIKE DOMINOES.
FOR:
LONG AGO –
YOU --
EVOLUTIONARILY –
COMPREHENDED –
ATTAINED –
EMBODIED –
THE:
FACT –
THE:

TRUTH:
THAT ALL OF THIS:
ENDLESS:
SPRAWL –
OF:
ANY ENVIRONMENT –
WORLDS –
DIMENSIONAL INFINITIES –
FRIENDS –
ENEMIES –
(THERE ARE NO ENEMIES!) –
ALL OF IT –
THE WHOLE –
SPRAWL –
OF IT –
IS ONLY –
A MIRROR –
OF WHO –
AND WHAT –
YOU:
ARE.

PART SEVEN

Randy just spent:
FIVE HOURS --
IN THROBBING:
BLISS.
We told him --
BECAUSE HE NEEDED TO HEAR:
"This is all you need to do --
TO MAKE ALL YOUR:
WILDEST:
DREAMS --
COME TRUE."
....
At the end of the fifth hour.
We are having Randy NOTICE:
This has not been a:
BLAST.
It has not been a:
TSUNAMI.
HE HAS NOT BEEN:
HOLDING ON FOR DEAR LIFE.
But *QUITE THE CONTRARY.*
This has been --
These FIVE HOURS have been --
THE REST OF RANDY'S LIFE WILL BE:
Just:
Really --

REALLY --

REALLY:

NICE.

And the *RESULTS* --

OH MY GOD THE RESULTS!

....

Once you find your HOME –

In your SELF –

YOU HAVE SOMETHING THAT MOST PEOPLE DON'T HAVE.

You have found –

SECURED –

A *TREASURE.*

If something WONDERFUL happens –

You say, "OK."

If something HORRENDOUS happens –

You say, "OK."

IT IS ALL YOU.

NOTHING CAN HAPPEN TO YOU THAT ISN'T:

YOU.

Randy just learned that one out of every twenty Americans owns an AR-15 semi-automatic rifle.

There was ANOTHER school shooting today.

RANDY CAN LOOK INTO THAT *MIRROR* AND SAY:

"OK."

UNITY –

Is a DISTINCTIVE love *ORIENTATION.*

It is more akin to COMPASSION –

Than to EROS.

THOUGH *LOOK OUT* WHEN THOSE GET INTERTWINED.

When you look at:

SOMEONE –

SOMETHING –

And RECOGNIZE –

REALIZE –

That you are looking AT –

And INTO:

YOURSELF –

IT WILL ALMOST ALWAYS BRING A TEAR TO YOUR EYE.

Even if that love *HAS* been EROTICIZED.

You want to say:

"THERE, THERE."

What MAKES THIS WORK –

What makes this:

VIABLE –

Is that you DO:

CONSISTENTLY –

FEEL THE SINOATRIAL *DRUMBEAT* –

PULSING THROUGHOUT YOUR ORGANISM.

You LOOK DOWN THERE –

And you DO SEE –

EXACTLY WHAT YOU WERE LOOKING AT IN YOUR WORLD.

WHO KNEW:

YOUR HEART;

HAD SO MANY:

SEMI-AUTOMATIC RIFLES:

IN IT.

Well.

IT DOES.

....

You are NO LONGER GUIDED BY:

"I WANT."

Well...

YOU ARE AND YOU AREN'T.

INCREASINGLY:

YOUR SELF *AT THE HIGHER ECHELONS* –

IS CALLING THE SHOTS.

Much of your *INTERPRETATION* –

Of CURRENT EVENTS –

INNER EVENTS –

AND YOU ARE NO LONGER FOOLED BY THE FALSE POLARITY OF INNER AND OUTER –

Is COMPREHENDED –

DEDUCED –

INTUITED –

SUSPECTED –

Based on:

HOW WELL YOU KNOW –

HOW CLOSELY ALIGNED YOU ARE –

HOW TRANSPARENT –

AND *SUBSUMED* –

YOU HAVE BECOME –

TO:

YOURSELF AT THE HIGHER ECHELONS.

THAT DIZZYING –
SWIRLING –
FOREVER SPEEDING UP:
EPSILON:
VORTEX –
THAT GOES UP TO:
FOREVER.
THE SAME *FOREVER* –
YOU FEEL PULSING –
IN YOUR VEINS –
AND *THROBBING* –
YOUR ENTIRE –
PHYSICAL –
ORGANISM.
Yes you are TRANSPARENT.
Yes you are:
SUBSUMED.
YES YOU STAY IN A CONTINUOUS –
PERMANENT –
STATE OF:
WOW.
You do wish it were:
EASIER.
But you DO NOT COMPLAIN.

IT IS HUMBLING AND THRILLING TO KNOW THAT YOU ARE ACTIVELY ENGAGED IN THE SAME BUSINESS OF UNIVERSE CONTINUANCE AND MAINTENANCE THAT THE GODHEAD TAKES IN STRIDE.

And you know –

OR AT LEAST *INTUIT* –

THAT THE REASON THE GODHEAD CAN TAKE *SUCH THINGS* IN STRIDE –

IS THAT:

THE GODHEAD:

DIES EASILY.

THE GODHEAD:

DIES CONTINUOUSLY.

IT DOES MAKE YOU FEEL *LESS LONELY* –

WHEN YOU –

CATCH YOURSELF:

DYING.

....

Something wonderful is happening.

And it isn't WISHFUL THINKING.

IT IS COMING FROM DEEP INSIDE YOURSELF.

Because that is where you are *LIVING FROM* NOW --

From DEEP INSIDE YOURSELF.

Notice:

THE PEOPLE AROUND YOU ARE MEETING YOU --

IN THAT PLACE DEEP INSIDE YOURSELF --

FROM DEEP INSIDE:

THEMSELVES.

The HEART.

The *HEART:*

BURSTING --

And EXPLODING --

With LOVE --

And LIGHT.

That *PLACE* --

DEEP WITHIN THE HEART OF GOD.

THE:

DEEP PLACE --

WITHIN ALL OF YOU --

THAT YOU ALL:

SHARE.

Even SWEET ROJI --

WITH HIS LITTLE HEAD RESTING ON YOUR CHEST NOW --

PURRING.

MEMORIES --

They come and go --

And they are all welcome.

THEY ARE ALL WELCOME.

NOTICE:

EVERYONE IS WELCOME.

NOTICE:

EVERYONE IS:

ALREADY HERE.

IN THIS PLACE --

DEEP WITHIN YOURSELF --

THAT YOU ALL SHARE.

The CONNECTIONS --

DON'T HAVE TO BE MADE.

BECAUSE THEY ARE:

ALREADY THERE.

EVERYONE:

READING THESE BOOKS --
IS ALREADY HERE.
NO SOLICITATIONS:
NECESSARY.
THE HEART --
YOUR HEART --
EVERYONE'S HEART --
THE HEART OF:
ALL THAT IS --
IS ALREADY:
HERE.
EITHER IT IS HERE --
OR IT IS NOT.
AND IT:
IS.
....
You have never felt CONNECTED --
TO EVERYONE --
LIKE THIS --
BEFORE.
NONE OF THIS HAS TO BE:
PLANNED OUT.
NONE OF THIS HAS TO BE:
LEARNED.
OR REHEARSED.
THIS:
KNOWLEDGE --
IS *NATIVE* --

HERE.
IN THIS DEEP PLACE --
WITHIN YOURSELF --
WHERE EVERYONE:
IS.
YOU HAVE:
SKILLS --
YOU NEVER KNEW YOU HAD.
YOU HAVE --
SOCIAL SKILLS --
SOCIAL GRACES --
YOU DIDN'T KNOW YOU HAD.
THAT YOU NEVER HAD BEFORE.
YOU JUST --
AND I MEAN *JUST NOW* --
ACQUIRED THEM.
IN THE FIFTH HOUR --
OF THIS AFTERNOON'S:
MEDITATION.
IT'S LIKE:
LIFETIMES --
EONS --
OF:
SOCIAL GRACES --
GOT TRANSFERED --
FULL-BLOWN --
INSTANTANEOUSLY --
DOWNLOADED --

LIKE:

WHERE DID THAT COME FROM?

YOU SEE YOURSELF --

SAILING --

FLOATING --

THROUGH PARTIES --

GRACIOUS --

WELCOMING --

GENEROUS --

REMEMBERING EVERYONE'S NAME.

MAKING EVERY GUEST FEEL LIKE THEY ARE THE MOST IMPORTANT PERSON THERE.

YOU SUPPOSE IT MUST BE SOME:

UNSOLICITED ---

BUT LONG HOPED-FOR:

SIDDHI --

A SPONTANEOUS GIFT --

THAT HAPPENS --

WHEN YOU GET --

TO WHERE YOU HAVE GOTTEN --

IN THIS FIFTH HOUR --

OF THIS AFTERNOON'S:

MEDITATION.

....

You'll take it.

It is a RESPONSIBILITY.

But more than that --

IT IS A FULL-ON JOY.

IN YOUR OWN HEART.

BUT EVEN MORE THAN THAT --
IN THE HEARTS --
OF THESE SWIRLING MASSES --
WHO DO SEEM TO:
LIGHT UP --
WHEN YOU:
SHOW UP --
WITH THIS HEART --
OF YOURS --
THAT IS --
SOMEHOW --
SUDDENLY --
AS OF THE FIFTH HOUR --
OF THIS AFTERNOON'S:
MEDITATION --
BIG ENOUGH --
OMNIPRESENT --
ENOUGH --
TO NOT ONLY HOLD --
BUT:
BE:
ALL THESE OTHER --
COUNTLESS --
SWIRLING --
SUDDENLY --
LIT-UP:
HEARTS.
WHICH IN TURN --

LIGHTS UP YOUR OWN HEART --
LIKE A:
SUPERNOVA.
NOT ONLY IS THIS A:
WHOLE NEW KIND OF:
LIGHT --
IT IS A:
WHOLE NEW KIND OF:
LOVE.
AND YES:
YOU'LL TAKE IT.
AND EVEN MORE IMPORTANTLY:
YOU WILL:
GIVE IT.
NOW THAT YOU CAN.
NOW THAT YOU:
HAVE IT TO GIVE.
AS OF THE:
FIFTH HOUR --
OF TODAY'S:
MEDITATION.

PART EIGHT

What we are doing is still HO'OPONOPONO.
We just aren't calling it that anymore.
This is quieter. Deeper.
There are no phrases.
The LAST FIVE HOURS have been WORDLESS --
Except our:
YES YES YES!
When you asked if we wanted you to:
GO FOR THE FIFTH HOUR.
The direction has changed.
From OUTER to INNER.
From UP to DOWN.
From FLYING to FALLING.
From ACQUIRING to DIVESTING.
From DOING to NOT DOING.
From GOALS to LETTING GO.
From DESIRING to SERVING.
From WORDS to:
SILENT OMNISCIENCE.
....
You wonder if there will be anything LEFT.
Our answer?
Maybe not.
The SPHERE OF ACTIVITY --
Has SHIFTED.
RELOCATED.

WHERE THERE USED TO BE:

SOMETHING --

THERE WILL BE NOTHING.

AND WHERE THERE USED TO BE:

NOTHING --

THERE WILL BE:

EVERYTHING.

YOU DIDN'T THINK YOU'D BE CONTINUING LIFE AS BEFORE, DID YOU?

....

The biggest SHIFT --

The biggest *RELOCATION* --

Will be from:

CARING --

To:

NOT CARING.

OH YOU'LL CARE.

JUST NOT ABOUT ANYTHING YOU USED TO CARE ABOUT.

LET'S SAY YOUR:

VALUES --

HAVE RELOCATED.

....

YOU WILL BE WALKING DOWN DIFFERENT STREETS.

IN DIFFERENT TOWNS.

WITH NEW FRIENDS.

MANY OF YOUR NEW FRIENDS --

WILL BE YOUR --

OLD FRIENDS --

RELOCATED.

OR AT LEAST YOU'LL SUSPECT THAT'S WHO THEY ARE.

YOU DON'T TAKE ANYTHING FOR GRANTED ANYMORE.

NOT EVEN WHAT YOU --

USED TO THINK YOU KNEW.

YOU ARE FINDING THAT:

CERTITUDE --

ISN'T AS USEFUL AS IT USED TO BE.

PROOF --

EVIDENCE --

CONVINCING --

THESE ARE NO LONGER RELEVANT.

NOT KNOWING --

HAS BECOME THE NEW:

GOLD STANDARD.

THE REQUIREMENT.

THE:

KEY --

THAT WILL GET YOU WHERE YOU NEED TO.

YOU ARE GETTING --

HAVE GOTTEN --

SUBSUMED ---

TO THE *HIGHER ECHELONS* OF WHO YOU ARE.

YOU --

HAVE--

A NEW:

YOU.

....

Randy is ENJOYING *FALLING*.

He has TURNED HIS BOAT AROUND –

And *THROWN THE OARS OVERBOARD*.

NO MORE *PADDLING UPSTREAM* FOR HIM.

Of course this is the general TREND now.

PLANETARILY SPEAKING NOW:

WHAT YOU'VE BEEN DOING HASN'T WORKED.

THERE ACTUALLY IS A:

MASS DECISION NOW –

To:

STOP PADDLING UPSTREAM AND THROW YOUR OARS OVERBOARD.

Of course this is SCARY.

BUT NOT AS SCARY AS THE SCENARIO YOU SEE IF YOU DO *NOT* CHANGE DIRECTIONS.

I want to emphasize:

THIS IS NOT A "CHOICE."

"CHOICE" IS PART OF THE *WELTANSCHAUUGAN* YOU ARE THROWING OVERBOARD.

Essentially –

There are TWO WAYS –

TO GET WHERE YOU ARE GOING.

THE EASY WAY –

AND THE HARD WAY.

THE *HARD WAY* CONSISTS OF:

TRYING.

PLANNING.

THINKING.

FIGURING OUT.

CHOOSING.

FREE WILL.

CREATING YOUR OWN REALITY –

AND ALL OF THAT NONSENSE.

IN A NUTSHELL:

EGO.

IT IS A NECESSARY EVOLUTIONARY STAGE.

DON'T FRET OVER IT.

THE *CORRECTION* IS BUILT IN.

IT DOESN'T TAKE MUCH TO SHATTER AN EGO.

ONCE –

RANDY LOST HIS PHONE –

AND DIED A MILLION DEATHS OVER IT.

There is an:

UNSPOKEN CONTROVERSY SWIRLING AROUND –

AND CONFOUNDING –

YOUR WORLD NOW.

LIKE:

OK. WE GET THE ANALOGY.

WE'RE ON A RIVER.

WE HAVE BEEN FIGHTING THIS RIVER WITH EVERY FIBER OF OUR BEING FOR MILLENIA.

THAT IS ESSENTIALLY WHAT –

CULTURE –

HAS BEEN.

CIVILIZATION.

LAWS.

RELIGIONS –

EVEN THE "BEST" OF THEM.

(Notice the quotes!)

BUT:

THE CONUNDRUM IS:

WHAT –

EXACTLY –

LIES –

DOWNSTREAM?

IS IT:

HEAVEN?

OR:

DESTRUCTION?

……..

There is ABSOLUTELY –

An element of COERCION here.

A HERD OF CATTLE GETTING CORRALLED INTO THE SLAUGHTER HOUSE.

WHEN THERE ARE NO CHOICES –

YOU TAKE THE –

ONLY –

"CHOICE" –

THAT IS AVAILABLE TO YOU.

THE FEAR IS REAL.

AND CANNOT BE WHITEWASHED.

THANK GOD YOU DO NOT WHITEWASH ANYTHING NOW.

YOU HAVE LEARNED TO –

HONOR –

YOURSELF.

VALIDATE YOURSELF.
VALIDATE YOUR EMOTIONS.
YOUR *REASONING* –
HOWEVER LIMITED IT MIGHT BE.
YOU DO NOT LET ANYONE *BULLY YOU* –
INTO THINKING YOU *POSSIBLY COULD* –
KNOW SOMETHING THAT YOU –
OBVIOUSLY –
DO NOT.
....
LIKING YOURSELF –
IS NO LESS –
THAN AN:
EVOLUTIONARY WONDER.
YOU NOW HAVE –
A TREASURE –
THAT IS HARD IN THE WINNING:
INTEGRITY.
YOU ARE:
IN LOVE.
HOW COULD YOU NOT BE?
ESPECIALLY WHEN YOU *MEDITATE* –
AS MUCH AS YOU DO.
YOU:
KNOW –
FIRSTHAND –
THE GLORIES OF:
ELYSEUM.

FOR THAT IS NOW YOUR:
DOMICILE.
……..
IT IS ALL ABOUT:
ANATOMY.
EARTH BODIES –
SEE EARTHLY THINGS.
LIGHT BODIES –
SEE:
LIGHT.
THE FACT OF THE MATTER IS:
IT DOESN'T MATTER WHAT YOU DO.
IT REALLY DOESN'T.
PADDLE UPSTREAM OR NOT –
IT REALLY DOESN'T MATTER.
IT DOESN'T MATTER WHAT YOU SAY.
YOU CAN CURSE LIKE SHAKESPEARE –
AND SAINT PETER WILL OPEN THE GATES FOR YOU –
WIDE.
IF –
AND I MEAN:
IF:
HE LIKES WHAT HE SEES.
YOU REALLY DO NEED TO THROW ALL OF YOUR –
CONCEPTS –
AND *CONCEPTUALIZATIONS* –
OVERBOARD.
OUT THE WINDOW.

INTO THE GARBAGE HEAP.
IT REALLY –
AND TRULY --
DOESN'T MATTER –
WHAT YOU DO.
OR SAY.
WHAT *MATTERS:*
IS WHAT:
YOU:
ARE.
....
And by that I mean:
WHAT *SPECIES* –
YOU:
ARE.
....
You don't know what you're doing.
BUT YOU'RE DOING IT.
You don't know where you're going –
BUT YOU'RE WELL ON YOUR WAY.
Not only is your ANATOMY *ENTIRELY NEW* –
SO IS YOUR LANDSCAPE.
YOUR TERRAIN.
THE ENTIRE SCHEMATA –
FRAMEWORK –
BULWARK –
UNDERPINNINGS –
ARE CATEGORICALLY:

UNFAMILIAR.

THE MULTIDIMENSIONALITY MAKES THEM SEEM *MASSIVE.*

CAVERNOUS.

YOU FEEL LIKE AN ANT IN A CATHEDRAL.

AND YES –

THE *HOLINESS* OF IT ALL DOES:

TAKE YOUR BREATH AWAY.

It's not like you'd rather be SOMEWHERE ELSE.

YOU *LIKE IT*, ACTUALLY.

The BIGGEST ABYSS –

In this UNEXPECTED *MEGALITH* –

Is the YAWNING *CRAVASSE* OF:

DEATH.

And yet.

DEATH IS SIMPLY PART OF THE FRAMEWORK.

This SKELETON is made up of BEAMS AND GIRDERS.

There are ELEVATORS.

TAKING YOU HIGH INTO THE SKY –

AND INTO THE DEPTHS OF WHAT YOU ONCE CALLED HELL.

Hell is simply UNFINISHED BUSINESS.

And you have learned –

AS HAS EVERYONE AT THIS PARTICULAR EVOLUTIONARY STAGE –

That BUSINESS CAN BE SETTLED.

Might take *EONS* of LIFETIMES.

A WIDE ARRAY OF INTERWOVEN –

INTERLOCKING –

DIMENSIONAL LEARNING OPPORUNITIES –

CURRICULA –

WITH PROFESSORS SO ADVANCED YOU ARE NOT EVEN ALLOWED TO SEE THEIR FACES.

(You have come to SUSPECT –

THEY DO NOT HAVE FACES.)

But yes.

WOUNDS –

HURTS –

GRIEVANCES –

KARMA –

CAN BE:

FORGIVEN.

ESPECIALLY WHEN YOU GRASP THAT EVERYTHING THAT ANYONE DID –

INCLUDING YOURSELF –

WAS ABSOLUTELY NECESSARY –

AND THAT NONE OF IT WAS A CHOICE .

SIMPLY:

REALITY WORKING ITSELF OUT.

Sentient beings –

EVEN ONES WITH BEYOND GENIUS-LEVEL BRILLIANCE –

ARE SIMPLY:

NATURAL PHENOMENA.

APPLES FALLING FROM TREES.

COMETS SHOOTING ACROSS THE HEAVENS.

WATER TURNING INTO ICE –

OR FALLING FROM THE SKY –

OR FLOODING ENTIRE CITIES WHILE THE CITIZENS DROWN IN THEIR OWN HOMES.

NO BLAME IS ASSIGNED.

NO RETRIBUTIVE LEGISLATION.

JUST REALITY WORKING ITSELF OUT.

FOR THAT IS WHAT WE ARE.

REALITY WORKING ITSELF OUT.

AND HAVING THE SAME CONFIDENCE AS AN ACORN –

THAT IT WILL.

....

So yes.

OBVIOUSLY:

HOW YOU CONSIDER OTHERS –

AND HOW YOU CONSIDER YOURSELF –

Has been:

REVOLUTIONIZED.

YOU:

ARE:

REALITY WORKING ITSELF OUT.

SO ARE YOUR FELLOWS.

NO BLAME.

YOU WOULDN'T CONSIDER YOURSELF A *SCIENTIST* –

BUT YOU HAVE ACQUIRED THE:

COLD HARD EYES OF ONE.

It is all simply DATA.

UTTERLY FASCINATING DATA.

YOU APPRECIATE THE:

TWIST OF IRONY.

THIS WIDE-OPEN –
SKY-OPEN:
HEART –
THAT YOU HAVE:
ACQUIRED –
(MUCH LIKE PUBESCENT SEXUAL ORGANS) –
PRECLUDES:
JUDGMENT.
ALL IS SEEN.
ALL IS ACCEPTED.
ALL IS –
FOR WANT OF A BETTER WORD:
LOVED.
AN OPEN HEART –
TURNS OUT –
DOES NECESSITATE –
THE COLD HARD-EYED FASCINATION –
OF A SCIENTIST.
Let's call it here the:
OBSERVER.
LET'S CALL IT WHAT IT IS.
NO MATTER WHO –
OR WHAT –
AND IT SEEMS NOW THAT THERE IS SCANT DIFFERENCE BETWEEN:
A WHO AND A WHAT –
BUT NEVERTHELESS –
THIS *FASCINATION* –
IS ENDLESSLY MESMERIZING.

All is ACCEPTED.
And all is:
INNATELY –
INCONTROVERTIBLY:
THRILLING.
LEARNING TO SEE ONESELF –
AS WELL AS OTHERS –
AS A:
WHAT –
SEEMS TO BE WHAT MAKES THIS WHOLE NEW:
ONTOLOGICAL ECOSYSTEM:
WORK.

PART NINE

All those things you think you want?

TURNS OUT YOU DON'T WANT THEM

AS MUCH AS YOU THINK YOU DO.

Do you really want:

FIFTY BILLION DOLLARS?

A MANSION?

A LAMBORGHINI?

I can tell you with ABSOLUTE *CERTITUDE:*

YOU DO NOT.

I'll give you a brief BUT *SUCCINCT* --

LESSON IN PHYSICS.

Your INNER SELF --

SPONTANEOUSLY CREATES:

YOUR BODY --

AND:

YOUR WORLD.

You don't have to worry about that.

It TAKES CARE OF ITSELF.

Our VERY FIRST TEACHING was:

EVERYONE ALWAYS GETS EXACTLY WHAT THEY WANT.

Again:

YOU DON'T HAVE TO WORRY ABOUT IT.

IT HAPPENS ALL BY ITSELF.

Another ORIGINAL TEACHING of ours is:

THE MIRACLE IS WHAT'S IN FRONT OF YOUR FACE.

If you are familiar with the DOUBLE SLIT EXPERIMENT --

You know that:

PHYSICAL REALITY ONLY EXISTS WHEN YOU ARE LOOKING AT IT.

Not only is WHAT IS IN FRONT OF YOUR FACE --

EXACTLY WHAT YOU ARE WANTING RIGHT NOW --

IT IS --

LITERALLY --

THE ONLY REALITY YOU HAVE.

What is RIGHT IN FRONT OF YOUR FACE --

Is a DIRECT COMMUNICATION from your:

INNER SELF.

Because this *IS* --

AFTER ALL --

NOT ONLY A RELATIONSHIP...

IT IS THE RELATIONSHIP YOU HAVE BEEN LOOKING FOR --

YOUR WHOLE LIFE.

It is a:

LOVE RELATIONSHIP.

Not only are you being:

GIVEN EXACTLY WHAT YOU WANT --

You are being:

TAUGHT *EXACTLY WHAT YOU NEED TO LEARN.*

....

Randy is in the process of publishing his fifth book:

GLORIOUS.

A friend of his is his BEST PROOFREADER.

But she has been sick and may not be able to proof *Glorious.*

Randy momentarily *PANICKED.*

Until we told him:

"YOU HAVE A PH.D.

I THINK YOU CAN PROOF A BOOK."

At this, RANDY LAUGHED.

He also wonders:

"ARE MY BOOKS SELLING ENOUGH?

DO I NEED A NEW MARKETING STRATEGY?

SHOULD I BE SPEAKING AT BARNES & NOBLE?"

Randy's second book *Salvo* --

Was a #1 best seller on Amazon in FIVE CATEGORIES --

And #2 in the category of PHILOSOPHY.

It outsold:

DEEPAK CHOPRA --

BRIAN WEISS --

DON MIGUEL RUIZ --

JANE GOODALL --

And even:

MARCUS AURELIUS.

Randy has a publicist, Monica --

He is TOTALLY IN LOVE WITH.

He has a publisher that is:

HAPPY TO PUBLISH HIS BOOKS --

AS FAST AS HE CAN WRITE THEM --

Which is averaging:

TWO A YEAR.

When you sit around --

WANTING --

SOMETHING YOU DO NOT HAVE --
YOU ARE TOTALLY:
MISSING THE BOAT.
This is a PROMISE I CAN MAKE CONFIDENTLY --
AND CATEGORICALLY:
WHAT IS RIGHT IN FRONT OF YOUR FACE --
IS A *MILLION TIMES BETTER* --
THAN WHAT YOU *THINK* --
YOU WANT --
INSTEAD.
LORD HAVE MERCY!
THE TROUBLE YOU CAUSE YOURSELF!
THE MIRACLE IS RIGHT IN FRONT OF YOUR FACE.
ALL YOU NEED TO DO TO SEE IT IS:
OPEN YOUR EYES.
Well...
In all fairness:
You may need *SOMEONE* --
FROM THE HIGHER ECHELONS --
TO POINT IT OUT TO YOU.
But guess what?
WE ARE HERE!
JUMPING UP AND DOWN!
WAVING OUR ARMS!
YELLING AT YOU --
TO ASK US.
....
Randy is in love with a man who lives in North Carolina --

Two hundred miles away.
This man is a sadhu.
A SAINT.
With IMPRESSIVE --
OTHERDIMENSIONAL CONNECTIONS --
AND CREDENTIALS.
He is an UNCANNY:
TWIN FLAME.
The day Randy met this man he did:
LAY IT ON THE LINE.
"I find you extremely attractive.
But if you propositioned me --
I'd have to:
POLITELY DECLINE.
I'd tell you:
'WE CAN DO WAY BETTER THAN THAT.'"
This man smiled knowingly and responded:
"WE ALREADY ARE."
There was a twinkle --
THAT IS STILL TWINKLING.
There was a kiss.
There was a hand on an ass.
THERE WERE *SPARKS* FLYING ALL OVER THE PLACE.
THERE WERE HALTING --
CHOKING --
INVITATIONS TO LIVE TOGETHER.
FOLLOWED BY HALTING --
CHOKING --

YESES.
THERE WERE CONSTITUTIONAL --
CHARACTEROLOGICAL --
IDEOLOGICAL COLLISIONS.
THERE WERE HOURS AND DAYS AND MONTHS --
OF SINCERE --
MUTUAL --
AND *SUCCESSFUL* --
HO'OPONOPONO PRAYERS OF FORGIVENESS.
THESE TWO MEN ARE CONSTELLATIONS.
SHOOTING CUPID'S ARROWS AT EACH OTHER --
HONESTLY HAVING THE TIME OF THEIR LIVES.
THEY WRITE SCRIPTURE TO EACH OTHER --
DAILY.
THE RESULTANT *COSMOLOGICAL COMBUSTION* --
AND ALL --
IT ACCOMPLISHES --
SEEN AND UNSEEN --
IS --
FOR THE MOST PART --
FAR BEYOND THEIR PRESENT PERCEPTUAL RANGE.
But:
THEY KNOW.
OH YES THEY KNOW.
WITHOUT NEEDING TO --
OR BEING ABLE TO --
BEGIN TO ARTICULATE IT:
THAT THEY ARE *DOING GOD'S WORK.*

AND SOOTHING:
ANCIENT:
ACHES.
This is not what they wanted.
BUT OH MY GOD IT:
ABSOLUTELY:
IS.

PART TEN

Eventually you'll figure out:
IT ISN'T ANYBODY'S FAULT.
NOBODY DID ANYTHING WRONG.
"CHOICE " IS AN ILLUSION.
You will need to start seeing:
YOURSELF --
AND EVERYBODY ELSE --
AS:
NATURAL PHENOMENA.
WATER TURNING INTO ICE --
OR FALLING FROM THE SKY.
LIGHT TRAVELLING LIGHT YEARS --
FROM THE FAR REACHES OF THE GALAXY.
AN ACORN BECOMING AN OAK TREE.
MORNING DEW.
You will need to begin seeing:
YOURSELF --
AND EVERYBODY ELSE --
AS A:
WHAT --
RATHER THAN AS A:
WHO.
A NATURAL PHENOMENON --
FOLLOWING:
NATURAL LAWS.
COULD AN APPLE TREE --

"DECIDE" --
TO PRODUCE ORANGES?
YOU:
DO WHAT YOU DO --
AND THAT IS THE ONLY THING THAT YOU --
COULD --
DO.
The *LIE* --
Of FREE WILL --
Is just a CONTINUATION --
Of your SUNDAY SCHOOL --
GOOD AND EVIL SILLINESS.
Another EXCUSE --
To BEAT YOURSELF --
Or SOMEONE ELSE --
UP.
Or to ARBITRARILY --
PRAISE:
YOURSELF --
OR SOMEONE ELSE --
For LIVING UP --
To some MADE-UP --
STANDARD.
ARE YOU REALLY SO:
STINGY --
YOU CAN'T SIMPLY --
ACCEPT --
AND AFFIRM --

THAT EVERYONE --
INCLUDING YOU --
IS DOING EXACTLY WHAT THEY NEED TO BE DOING?
EXACTLY WHAT THEY ARE:
SUPPOSED --
TO BE DOING?
....
What is this need you have --
To make YOURSELF --
AND OTHERS --
AND YOUR WORLD --
WRONG?
I CAN SPEAK WITH AUTHORITY HERE:
THE ONLY THING “WRONG” HERE --
IS YOUR OBSESSION --
WITH MAKING:
YOURSELF --
AND OTHERS --
AND YOUR:
WORLD --
WRONG.
And of course:
ULTIMATELY;
EVEN THAT --
ISN’T:
WRONG.
IT IS SIMPLY:
YOU --

ON YOUR:
CONVOLUTED JOURNEY --
FROM:
CATERPILLAR --
TO BUTTERFLY.
....
WHAT A RELIEF IT WILL BE --
WHEN YOU CAN GRASP --
THAT:
EVERYONE IS DOING --
EXACTLY WHAT THEY ARE SUPPOSED --
TO BE DOING.
YOU ARE DOING --
EXACTLY WHAT *YOU* --
ARE SUPPOSED TO BE DOING.
AND THE WORLD --
IS DOING --
EXACTLY --
WHAT --
IT --
IS SUPPOSED TO BE DOING.
THEN YOU WILL SEE --
YOU WILL KNOW --
THAT EVERYTHING HAS BEEN PERFECT --
ALL ALONG.
ALWAYS HAS BEEN --
ALWAYS WILL BE --
COULDN'T --

NOT --

BE.

....

We just asked Randy:

"WHAT ARE YOU FEELING?

He answered:

"My full body throb."

We said,

"RIGHT ANSWER."

Then we asked him:

"WHAT IS THE BEST POSITION TO DO MEDITATION IN?"

He said:

"Lying down in bed."

We responded:

"WRONG ANSWER.

THE BEST POSITION TO DO MEDITATION IN IS:

WHATEVER POSITION YOUR BODY HAPPENS TO BE IN."

We asked again:

"WHAT ARE YOU FEELING?
He answered:

"MY FULL BODY THROB."

We told him:

"EXCELLENT."

Then we asked:

"WHAT DOES AWARENESS OF THE FULL BODY THROB PRODUCE?"

He said:

"MAINTAINING AWARENESS OF THE FULL BODY THROB WILL MAKE ALL YOUR WILDEST DREAMS COME TRUE."

You see:

RANDY IS IN TRAINING TO BE AN:

OVERSOUL.

OVERSOUL ISN'T EXACTLY AN ELECTED POSITION.

NOR APPOINTED.

IT IS:

MERIT BASED.

WELL…

IT IS COMPETENCY BASED.

IT IS *ANATOMY BASED*.

YOU NEED TO HAVE THE RIGHT ANATOMY.

IT IS MUCH LIKE PUBERTY, IN THAT SENSE.

IN ORDER TO CONCEIVE A CHILD –

OR BEAR A CHILD –

ALL THE RIGHT "PARTS" MUST BE INTACT –

AND FUNCTIONAL.

RANDY'S ANATOMY IS NOW INTACT –

AND FUNCTIONAL.

……..

OVERSOUL DOES IMPLY A:

MULTIDIMENSIONALITY.

IT REQUIRES A:

WORKING KNOWLEDGE –

OF:

REINCARNATION.

AND PROBABILITIES.

AND THE *HIERACHY* OF ECHELONS.

IT REQUIRES –

NOT ONLY THE KNOWLEDGE –

AND FAMIARITY –

OF THE TEN BASIC DIMENSIONS –

BUT ALSO:

VERIFIABLE *CITIZENSHIP* –

IN EACH OF THEM.

RANDY COULD OPEN UP HIS WALLET RIGHT NOW AND SHOW YOU:

THE TEN *LICENSES* –

LIKE A DRIVERS'S LICENSE.

OR DIPLOMAS –

LIKE HAVING:

TEN DOCTORAL DEGREES.

NEEDLESS TO SAY:

HIS WALLS ARE FULL OF THEM.

LET'S JUST SAY:

HE HAS GOTTEN HIS PICURE ON THE FRONT PAGE OF HIS LOCAL NEWSPAPER –

OFTEN ENOUGH –

THAT THE AVERAGE CITIZEN MUST SUPPOSE THAT HE IS *MAYOR* –

OR AT LEAST CITY MANAGER.

PERHAPS SHERIFF.

BUT HE IS NOT MAYOR, OR CITY MANAGER, OR SHERIFF.

WHAT HE IS:

IS A:

BURGEONING:
OVERSOUL.
....
The TECHNICAL COMPLEXITY –
Of this:
COVETED POSITION –
RENDERS IT:
CONCEPTUALLY UNWEILDY –
FOR THE AVERAGE CITIZEN.
NOT TO MENTION:
DAUNTING.
IT'S NOT LIKE YOU CAN BECOME AN:
OVERSOUL –
JUST BECAUSE YOU WANT TO.
IN FACT:
YOU MIGHT VERY MUCH *NOT* WANT TO –
AND YET EFFECTIVELY:
HAVE NO CHOICE.
RANDY DID *NOT* –
WECOME PUBERTY.
HE KNEW IT WOULD NECESSITATE AN:
IMMERSION –
NOT ONLY IN:
HUMANITY –
CREATUREHOOD –
BUT IN FACT ITS:
DARKEST FEATURES.
THIS HE DID NOT RELISH.

His REACTION was:

"OH GOD. DID I REALLY SIGN UP FOR THIS?"

THE REALITY –

OF COURSE –

WAS *FAR WORSE* –

THAN HIS:

WORST FEARS.

RECENTLY RANDY HAS WATCHED VIDEOS OF ANIMALS COPULATING.

He was most struck by:

FIRST THERE IS SNIFFING.

AND THEN THE *ATTACK*.

WITHOUT ANY REGARD WHATSOEVER –

FOR THE PARTNER'S WISHES –

OR WELLBEING.

LIKE A KIND OF DEMONIC POSSESSION.

He felt:

OVERWHELMING COMPASSION –

For not only the hapless *VICTIM* of these ASSAULTS –

But perhaps most of all for the AGGRESSORS –

Who are THEMSELVES –

HAPLESS VICTIMS OF A WHOLE OTHER –

INTERNAL –

INTRAPSYCHIC –

HORMONAL --

ASSAULT.

....

But Randy SURVIVED –

His PUBERTY –

IF BARELY!
HE ALSO SURVIVED HIS:
SECOND PUBERTY –
IN HIS FORTIES AND FIFTIES –
COURTESY OF:
CRYSTAL METH –
VIAGRA –
A LUCRATIVE CAREER AS A:
SEX WORKER --
AND PERHAPS MOST OF ALL:
FROM HIS *ABDUCTION* BY AN:
INSANELY –
LIBIDINOUS –
DEITY.
When sex is your *RELIGION* –
I can promise you:
THERE WILL BE A LOT OF IT.
……..
He is glad all of that is over.
The new *REQUIREMENT* –
Of being:
SINGLE –
CELIBATE –
And:
ABSTINENT –
Is:
TRULY:
FAR:

PREFERABLE.
....
You see:
BASE DESIRES –
DO NOT GET:
WAIVED –
ESCAPED FROM –
RENOUNCED.
No.
THEY:
GET:
SATISFIED.
QUENCHED.
SATIATED.
FULFILLED.
TWO DECADES –
OF INDULGENT –
NONSTOP SEX –
REALLY DOES –
DO THE TRICK:
QUITE NICELY.
And yes –
As WONDROUS –
As it WAS:
You're glad it's over.
YOU DON'T MISS IT.
You're proud of it –
LIKE ALL THOSE DIPLOMAS ON YOUR WALLS –

But your attitude is:

THANK GOD I DON'T HAVE TO DO THAT AGAIN.

And you don't.

It is FINISHED.

YOU:

GRADUATED.

....

Understandably –

PREDICTABLY –

AFTER ALL THAT:

Your turn:

INWARD.

You start:

TENDING –

INWARD.

NOTICING:

INWARD.

You take up:

MEDITATION.

You notice:

Your:

URGES –

ARE JUST AS STRONG –

AS THEY ALWAYS WERE.

JUST:

INSTEAD OF DIRECTING THEM *OUTWARD* –

You now –

BECAUSE YOU HAVE EXHAUSTED ALL OTHER AVENUES –

DIRECT THEM:
INWARD –
AND:
UP.
....
Turns out –
THERE ARE WELCOMING –
LOVERS –
A-PLENTY –
INSIDE –
AND UP.
You find a *HEART.*
You've always –
VAGUELY –
BEEN AWARE –
OF THE STEADY:
DRUMBEAT.
EVEN THE:
FULL BODY:
THROB.
And then one:
FORTUITOUS –
DAY:
YOU KNOCK ON THAT HEART –
AND THE DOOR OPENS –
AND YOU ENTER.
AND YOU FIND A:
VAST –

FULLY POPULATED:
WORLD.
INSIDE YOUR HEART.
And --
WOULDN'T YOU KNOW IT –
WHEN YOUR HEART OPENS TO:
YOU –
IT OPENS –
AUTOMATICALLY –
SIMULTANEOUSLY –
TO:
EVERYBODY –
AND EVERYTHING –
ELSE.
NOW YOUR HEART:
REALLY IS:
VASTLY –
INCOMPREHENSIVELY:
POPULATED.
In fact:
EVERYONE WHO:
EVER WAS –
IS NOW –
OR EVER WILL BE –
NOW CLAIMS –
NOT ONLY CITIZENSHIP –
BUT *RESIDENCY* –
INSIDE:

YOUR:
HEART.
....
How do you *FEED* –
THESE MASSES?
You notice everyone is:
LOOKING UP.
So YOU –
LOOK UP.
You see that –
ALL OF THE HIGHER DIMENSIONS ARE:
ALSO:
PROFUSELY POPULATED.
And just as you did with your:
WORLD'S POPULATION –
YOU OPEN YOUR HEART TO THEM.
TO ALL THE:
HIGHER DIMENSIONAL MASSES.
AND:
IN:
THEY:
COME!
....
SO NOW:
ALL THESE *EXTENSIVE POPULATIONS* –
FROM *ALL* OF THESE DIMENSIONS –
DO TEEM –
AND THRIVE –

AND *BURGEON* –
WITHIN:
YOUR:
OWN:
HEART.
YOU FIND IT PUZZLING –
AND HUMBLING –
BUT MOST OF ALL:
DELIGHTFUL –
SEEING THAT *MANY* OF THESE NEW:
RESIDENTS OF YOUR HEART –
ARE QUANTUMLY –
INCOMPREHENSIBLY –
MORE ADVANCED –
MORE EVOLVED –
MORE:
RESPLENDENT –
THAN YOU ARE.
And you know what you do?
You:
SMILE.
....
ALL OF THESE:
POPULATIONS –
CIVILIZATIONS –
HEIRARCHIES OF ECHELONS –
SPECIES –
NOW LIVE –

RESIDE –
CLAIM CITIZENSHIP –
THRIVE --
IN YOUR:
VERY:
OWN:
HEART.
YES.
WHEN YOU KNOCKED ON YOUR HEART –
AND THE DOOR OPENED –
AND YOU WENT INSIDE –
SO TOO –
DID:
ALL BEINGS EVERYWHERE:
WALK INSIDE –
CLAIM CITIZENSHIIP –
MAKE RESIDENCE –
THRIVE.
IT IS A LOVE YOU CAN'T:
ABDICATE –
RELENQUISH –
WALK AWAY FROM.
NO MATTER HOW MUCH YOU MIGHT WANT TO.
THINK OF IT AS A:
HIGHER DIMENSIONAL PUBERTY.
ALL THE:
PARTS:
THE *ORGANS* –

ARE THERE.
AND YOU KNOW VERY WELL:
IF YOU HAVE A SEXUAL ORGAN –
YOU'RE GOING TO USE IT –
SOMEHOW.
IT'S NOT GOING TO:
STAND IDLY BY –
AND BE IGNORED.
IT WILL –
MAKE SURE –
YOU NOTICE IT!
TURNS OUT THE:
HEART –
IS THE SAME WAY.
IT WILL *NOT* –
BE –
DENIED.
AND THAT IS HOW YOU BECOME AN:
OVERSOUL.
LIKE IT OR NOT.

PART ELEVEN

The causal body --
IS THE BODY OF POWER.
It is called the CAUSAL BODY --
BECAUSE IT MAKES THINGS HAPPEN.
WITHOUT ANY EFFORT WHATSOEVER.
Your WORLD --
SIMPLY --
AUTOMATICALLY --
APPEARS --
RATHER MAGICALLY --
As the:
CONTENTS OF YOUR CAUSAL BODY:
SPREAD OUT ACROSS THE HORIZON.
SPREAD OUT ACROSS THE LANDSCAPE.
SPREAD OUT:
AS:
YOUR *WORLD*.
But it is --
SIMPLY --
A MIRROR IMAGE --
AND HAS NO --
DETERMINATIVE --
REALITY --
OF ITS OWN.

The POWER --
Is in the BODY --
AND NOT IN THE WORLD.
We'll give you an image.
FLOWERS SPRING UP --
WITH EACH STEP.
DOORS OPEN --
AS YOU APPROACH THEM.
MONEY APPEARS --
AS YOU NEED IT.
LOVE APPEARS --
PRECISELY --
HOW --
AND WHEN --
YOU NEED IT.
Conversely --
BUT ACCORDING TO THE SAME PRINCIPLE --
LOVE WILL *RECEDE* --
VANISH --
WHEN ITS NEED HAS BEEN FULFILLED.
LIKEWISE:
MONEY WILL --
NOT --
PROLIFERATE --
WHEN THERE IS NO NEED.
LOVE AND MONEY --
WHEN NOT NEEDED --
ARE MERELY:

CLUTTER.
THE CAUSAL BODY --
IS A:
GOD --
THAT TAKES CARE OF YOU.
YOUR:
ENVIRONMENT --
IS:
HOW --
THIS GOD --
YOUR CAUSAL BODY --
TAKES CARE OF YOU.
BY MAKING THINGS --
MAGICALLY APPEAR --
WHEN THEY ARE NEEDED.
AND MAGICALLY:
DISAPPEAR --
WHEN THEY ARE NOT.

....

A couple of weeks ago we told Randy:
YOU NEED TO START MEDITATING --
FIVE HOURS --
IN THE AFTERNOON.
He was already meditating --
THREE OR FOUR HOURS --
So it was easy for him to say:
"Sure. Why not?"
One of the first things he noticed was this --

NEW BODY.
He didn't know what it was --
So we told him.
He already knew about the:
CAUSAL PLANE.
Years ago we'd told him:
THE CAUSAL PLANE --
IS WHAT YOU WOULD CALL:
HEAVEN ON EARTH .
THE FULFILLMENT OF ALL --
YOUR WILDEST DREAMS.
We said:
AND NOW YOU HAVE THE:
CAUSAL BODY --
TO MAKE THIS IS:
ACTUALLY:
OPERATIONAL.
We told him:
THIS:
IS:
THE MISSING PIECE.
....
One of the first things he noticed was:
BOTH THE PHYSICAL AND ASTRAL BODIES --
MOVE AROUND.
YOU DECIDE TO GO SOMEWHERE --
AND YOU GO.
The CAUSAL BODY:
STAYS:

STATIONARY.

IT IS THE CENTER OF THE UNIVERSE AND THE UNIVERSE REVOLVES AROUND IT.

IF THE CAUSAL BODY IS INCLINED --

TO GO TO SAN FRANCISCO --

IT LIES BACK IN ITS LAZY BOY CHAIR --

OR ON ITS BED--

AND *DOWNLOADS* --

A PROGRAM --

OF SAN FRANCISCO --

INTO THE:

VIRTUAL REALITY GOGGLE *HOLODECK SYSTEM* --

AND:

"GOES TO TOWN" --

SO TO SPEAK.

SAN FRANCISCO --

AND ALL OF ITS DELIGHTS --

COME TO HIM.

....

We've said before:

YOUR JOURNEY --

IS FROM THE HEAD --

TO:

THE HEART.

That is true.

AND I'LL GIVE YOU AN EVEN:

TRUER TRUTH.

YOUR JOURNEY:

IS FROM THE PHYSICAL/ASTRAL PLANES --

TO THE:
CAUSAL PLANE.
OF COURSE:
YOU CAN NOW:
DISCARD --
AND EFFECTIVELY --
MUST --
DISCARD --
YOUR:
PHYSICAL AND ASTRAL BODIES.
DON'T WORRY.
THEY WILL:
FALL AWAY --
OF THEIR OWN ACCORD --
LIKE A SNAKE --
SHEDDING ITS SKIN.
PERHAPS THE ONLY:
"TRICK" --
REQUIRED OF YOU --
WILL BE TO:
MEDITATE AN HOUR EXTRA.
THERE WILL NEED TO BE --
SOME KIND OF:
GESTURE --
OF WILLINGNESS --
COMMITMENT --
DECLARATION --
OF YOUR:

WORTHINESS --
SINCERITY --
EVOLUTIONARY:
CAPABILITY.
THESE:
EVOLUTIONARY *LEAPS* --
ARE ALWAYS:
RIFE --
WITH SYMBOLISM.
YOU'LL NOTICE:
THE AQUARIAN AGE --
IS AN EARTH-BASED:
RELIC.
USEFUL --
FROM THAT --
LIMITED --
MYOPIC --
PERSPECTIVE.
BUT YOU ARE IN THE:
FAR REACHES --
OF:
DEEP SPACE --
NOW.
THOSE:
PRIMITIVE:
BEARINGS --
ARE NO LONGER --
USEUL.

TRAINING WHEELS --
MUST BE --
KICKED AWAY.
ONCE YOUR:
CAUSAL BODY --
GETS:
ACTIVATED --
YOU WILL KNOW --
THAT YOU ARE IN A:
TIME --
AND SPACE --
WHERE THERE *IS NO:*
TIME AND SPACE.
EARTH BECOMES:
A MYTH.
A:
CREATION STORY.
A:
FAIRY TALE --
THAT YOU --
AND ALL THOSE LIKE YOU --
KNOW IN YOUR HEARTS --
NEVER HAPPENED.
WHICH MATTERS:
NOT:
ONE:
BIT.
IT DOESN'T MATTER --

WHERE YOU:
CAME FROM.
BECAUSE YOU:
LIKE:
WHERE:
YOU:
ARE.

....

Life just got MORE REAL.
THERE IS A --
REALITY --
THAT IS *MORE REAL* --
BY FAR --
THAN YOUR CURRENT 3D EARTH EXPERIENCE --
WHICH ISNT NEARLY AS REAL AS YOU THINK IT IS.
Think about it:
Your MOMENTS are so *FLEETING*.
THE INSTANT SOMETHING APPEARS --
IT VANISHES.
That was Seth's ORIGINAL TEACHING:
PHYSICAL REALITY HAS NO ENDURANCE.
You eat an apple --
OR MAKE LOVE --
AND FIVE MINUTES LATER YOURE ASKING:
"WHERE DID IT GO?"
And if you WANT MORE --
Well...
THERE MIGHT NOT BE ANY MORE.

It's a little TRICKY --

BUT I'LL EXPLAIN IT.

PHYSICAL REALITY IS DIRECTLY CREATED --

IS THE THEMATIC *OUTPICTURING* --

OF THE CAUSAL BODY.

So...

There is always a ONE ON ONE *DIRECT CORRELATION* --

BETWEEN THE CAUSAL PLANE --

AND THE PHYSICAL PLANE.

THEY ARE --

DIFFERENT.

BUT THEY ARE ALWAYS --

IN PERFECT:

AGREEMENT.

YOU DON'T NEED TO CHANGE THE WORLD --

BECAUSE IT'S ALREADY WHERE YOU WANT IT.

YOU DON'T HAVE TO CHANGE WHAT YOU'RE DOING --

BECAUSE WHAT YOU'RE DOING IS ALREADY PERFECT.

NOBODY ELSE NEEDS TO CHANGE WHAT THEY'RE DOING --

BECAUSE EVERYTHING THAT EVERYBODY ELSE IS DOING --

IS ALREADY PERFECT.

THE PERFECTION OF THE UNIVERSE IS NO LONGER A THEORY --

IT'S RIGHT IN FRONT OF YOUR FACE.

THE MOST OBVIOUS THING IN THE WORLD.

YOU DON'T HAVE TO WORRY ABOUT REALITY ANYMORE.

YOU DON'T EVEN HAVE TO THINK ABOUT IT ANYMORE.

IN FACT:

YOU DON'T HAVE TO --

THINK --

AT ALL.

IN FACT:

YOU --

WON'T --

THINK --

ANYMORE.

BECAUSE ON THE CAUSAL PLANE --

THERE IS:

NO:

THOUGHT.

THERE'S JUST:

NO NEED FOR IT.

ALL THERE *IS* IS:

YOU:

DOING --

BEING --

YOU.

AND YOUR WORLD IS JUST WHAT THAT LOOKS LIKE.

ALMOST:

AS A COURTESY.

AS IF SAYING:

"YES YOU ARE AS MAGNIFICENT AS THAT."

PART TWELVE

You are about to:
VACATE YOUR BODY.
AND WON'T THAT BE WONDERFUL!
Your heart is already:
OPEN SKY.
Your brain --
Your MIND --
Is OPEN SKY.
EVEN YOUR WORLD --
NOW --
IS OPEN SKY.
And now you're seeing that your:
BODY --
MUST ALSO BE:
OPEN SKY.
You LIKE --
OPEN SKY.
You --
PREFER --
OPEN SKY.
IN OPEN SKY --
THERE IS NO:
THOUGHT.
NO PLANS.

NO DESIRE.
NO PREFERENCE --
FOR ONE THING OVER ANOTHER.
THERE IS NO:
YOU.
AND THERE IS NO:
ME.
THERE IS NO:
HOPE.
YOU HAVE EMBRACED YOUR OWN --
SMALLNESS --
AND PETTINESS.
AND THE SMALLNESS AND PETTINESS --
OF EVERYONE ELSE.
EVERYONE --
INCLUDING YOU --
HAS BEEN:
LET OFF THE HOOK.
NO GOOD --
NO BAD.
NO PRAISE --
NO CONDEMNATION --
NO SUPERIORITY.
NO PUNISHMENT.
NO:
PLANS FOR:
IMPROVEMENT.
NO:
DESIRE TO:

MAKE THE WORLD A "BETTER PLACE."
NO SELF-RIGHTEOUS ZEAL --
TO:
SAVE THE WORLD.
OR TO HELP --
ANYONE.
NOT ONLY DO YOU --
SEE --
PERFECTION --
EVERYWHERE --
AND IN:
EVERYONE ...
YOU --
LITERALLY --
AND KNOWINGLY:
BRING --
PERFECTION.
YES.
THAT IS WHAT YOU BRING.
YOU:
BRING:
PERFECTION.
THAT IS YOUR:
CONTRIBUTION --
TO EVERYWHERE --
AND EVERYONE.
YOU DELIGHT --
IN ALLOWING --
ANYONE --

TO:
LOOK THROUGH YOUR EYES.
BECAUSE WHEN THEY --
LOOK THROUGH YOUR EYES --
THEY WILL:
SEE WHAT YOU SEE.
THAT'S WHAT THESE BOOKS ARE.
EVERYONE WHO --
READS THESE BOOKS --
WILL:
SEE WHAT I SEE.
EVERYONE NEEDS TO:
SEE WHAT I SEE.
EVERYONE NEEDS TO SEE --
THROUGH THE EYES --
OF THEMSELVES --
AT THE HIGHER ECHELONS.
AND THAT --
IS WHAT --
I AM.
....
Your body is the MIRACLE.
The MICROCOSM.
THAT'S where you do the WORK.
And then it SHOWS UP --
IN YOUR LIFE.
....
Randy just spent:
FIVE HOURS --

THROBBING.
With BOILING LIGHT.
It was GLORIOUS.
ECSTATIC.
HIGH-LEVEL MIRACULOUS.
THERE WAS NOTHING TO *FIX*.
JUST:
FLYING --
DIVING --
THROBBING --
THROUGH ENDLESS --
VAST --
CORRIDORS --
CAVERNS --
CANYONS --
Of *DEEP SPACE*.
The CAUSAL BODY --
IS:
VAST --
IN THIS WAY.
MONUMENTAL.
MEGALITHIC.
VEINS.
NEURONS
APERTURES.
CRANIOSACRAL MYELIN SHEATHS.
I CAN TELL YOU RIGHT NOW:
THIS IS WHAT HIS:
LIFE --

WILL LOOK LIKE.
BECAUSE:
ON THE CAUSAL PLANE --
THE WORLD JUST SHOWS YOU --
LIKE A PERFECT PICTURE --
A SNAPSHOT --
A PORTRAIT --
A LANDSCAPE --
OF WHAT'S HAPPENING --
THE:
STATE OF:
INSIDE:
YOUR BODY.
SO:
FLY THROUGH CANYONS AT WILL!
AND DO --
NOT --
WORRY ABOUT YOUR WORLD.
THE WORLD WILL BE THERE.
THE WORLD OF:
BLISS --
WILL BE THERE
THE WORLD OF:
GLORY --
WILL *BE THERE.*
THIS IS YOUR:
HOLY:
MAGICAL PRACTICE:
NOW.

DO IT AT WILL.
....
While THERE --
IN THOSE VAST CANYONS OF GLORY --
Randy saw BRIAN.
RANDY DID NOT CRY.
HE:
FLEW.
HE:
LEAPT --
WITH JOY.
THEY BOTH DID!
THEY FLEW --
THEY:
LEAPT:
IN JOY.
TOGETHER.
FUCK THE WORLD!
RANDY AND BRIAN --
LEAPT TOGETHER --
IN JOY.
AND FLEW --
AND FLEW --
AND *FLEW* --
TOGETHER.
LIKE THEY ALWAYS DID.

PART THIRTEEN

The CRYSTALLINE BODY is:
TRANSLUCENT.
At some point --
MAYBE AFTER FOUR OR FIVE --
HOURS OF MEDITATION --
It will *CLICK* --
Into place.
And yes you will HEAR --
OR MAYBE FEEL --
A "CLICK."
It reminds Randy of his first experience --
With HO'OPONOPONO.
AFTER SIX HOURS --
OF SAYING THE PHRASES --
A:
PEACE --
DESCENDED.
AND HE KNEW IT HAD DESCENDED FOR:
EVERYONE.
It was:
PALPABLE.
The following day --
The:
PEACE DESCENDED after:

EIGHT HOURS.
On the THIRD DAY --
Randy lay down to do --
MORE HO'OPONOPONO --
But we told him:
"NO .
THAT PRAYER HAS BEEN ANSWERED --
IN FULL."
Sometimes:
THINGS ARE ACCOMPLISHED --
AND THEY ARE:
ACCOMPLISHED.
ONCE AND FOR ALL.
ONCE YOUR CAUSAL BODY --
GETS *ACCOMPLISHED* --
YOU WILL KNOW IT --
AND EVERYONE ELSE WILL TOO.
You'll remember:
ALTHOUGH THE --
WORLD --
WILL ALWAYS BE A PERFECT:
REFLECTION --
OF THE:
CONTENTS --
OF YOUR CAUSAL BODY --
THE CAUSAL BODY WILL ALWAYS BE:
MORE:
REAL --
BY FAR.

THE CAUSAL BODY IS:
DETERMINATIVE.
ONCE YOUR CAUSAL BODY IS:
ACTIVATED --
YOU WILL KNOW IT --
AND EVERYBODY ELSE WILL TOO.
IT IS AN:
EVENT --
MORE PALPABLE BY FAR --
THAN ANYTHING PHYSICAL EVER COULD BE.
YOU --
AND EVERYONE AROUND YOU --
WILL GET:
FIRST-HAND EXPERIENCE --
OF HOW:
WISPY --
NEARLY IRRELEVANT --
PHYSICAL REALITY --
ACTUALLY IS.
....
Because the CAUSAL BODY --
ALWAYS CORRESPONDS --
PRECISELY --
WITH PHYSICAL REALITY --
IT IS:
BASIC.
BASE.
DISTINCTLY:

GROUNDED.
THE LIGHT EXPLODES --
AS RESPLENDENTLY AS EVER --
BUT THERE IS THIS:
GUT PUNCH --
FOOT STOMP --
GUN SHOT --
QUALITY TO THE CAUSAL PLANE --
THAT WILL KEEP YOU BREATHLESS.
YOU WILL BE ASTONISHED --
AND SO WILL EVERYONE AROUND YOU --
BY HOW *REAL* --
SOMETHING THAT IS NOT REAL AT ALL --
CAN BE.
YOU BEGIN TO WONDER:
IS PHYSICAL REALITY THE:
SAME AS --
THE CAUSAL PLANE?
IF THAT DOES TURN OUT TO BE THE CASE --
AND PERHAPS IT ALREADY HAS --
THEN I AM SURE --
THAT YOU WILL END UP CALLING IT:
THE CAUSAL PLANE --
AND NOT PHYSICAL PLANE.
YOU SEE:
YOU WERE RIGHT ALL ALONG!
PHYSICAL REALITY --
DOESN'T --
EXIST --

IN ANY --
MEANINGFUL --
WAY.
BUT THE CAUSAL PLANE--
OH MY FUCKING GOD IT DOES.
....
I remember --
The FIRST TIME --
WE DISCUSSED --
THE CAUSAL PLANE --
WITH RANDY --
WE TOLD HIM:
"THIS IS WHERE THE NOTION OF:
HEAVEN ON EARTH --
COMES FROM."
We continued:
"THE BEST DEFINITION OF:
THE CAUSAL PLANE --
WE CAN GIVE YOU --
IS THIS:
THE CAUSAL PLANE --
IS:
EVERY ONE OF YOUR WILDEST DREAMS --
COMING TRUE."
AS I RECALL --
THAT WAS OUR DEFINITION OF:
PHYSICAL REALITY --
TOO.

AND NOW YOU WILL SEE WHY.

....

But you see:

It is the CAUSAL *BODY* --

THAT MAKES THE:

ENTIRETY OF THE:

CAUSAL PLANE:

OPERATIONAL.

UNTIL THEN --

IT IS:

FASCINATING BUT:

THEORETICAL.

YOU SEE:

THERE IS A CRUCIAL --

WORLD OF DIFFERENCE --

BETWEEN:

ALL OF YOUR WILDEST DREAMS COMING TRUE AND --

ALL OF --

YOUR --

WILDEST DREAMS --

COMING TRUE.

WHEN YOUR --

ONCE YOUR --

OWN --

CAUSAL BODY --

POPS --

YOU WILL SEE WHAT I MEAN.

OH YES YOU WILL SEE WHAT I MEAN!

BECAUSE THEN YOU WILL BE:
LEAPING WITH JOY --
IN THE SAME WAY THAT YOU HAVE --
ALWAYS --
SEEN:
US --
LEAPING WITH JOY.
YOU WILL UNDERSTAND --
WHY --
WE ARE ALWAYS:
LEAPING WIYH JOY.
BECAUSE NOW YOU WILL BE LEAPING WITH JOY --
TOO.
IN FACT:
THE *DEFINING FEATURE* --
OF THE CAUSAL BODY --
IS THAT IT IS ALWAYS:
LEAPING WITH JOY.
....
Needless to say:
That was --
NOT --
The definition of:
PHYSICAL REALITY.
And that is WHY --
I THINK YOU WILL AGREE --
WE WILL CALL THIS STATE --
THE:

CAUSAL PLANE --
AND NOT THE:
PHYSICAL PLANE.
IT COMES DOWN TO THE:
DEFINING FEATURE:
LEAPING --
WITH --
JOY.

PART FOURTEEN

We just told Randy:
YOUR WRITING CAREER IS:
NOT --
IMPORTANT.
IT IS:
RESIDUE.
IT IS:
AFTERBIRTH.
IT IS:
REFUSE.
IT IS:
DROSS.
IT IS:
EXCREMENT.
LET IT HAPPEN.
IT IS THE:
TAIL END --
OF AN ORGANIC --
SACRED --
COSMOLOGICAL:
EVENT.
WHEN YOU MEDITATE --
AND WHEN YOU --
ALLOW YOURSELF TO:

DO:
WHAT YOU WERE:
ALREADY DOING --
NOW *THAT*:
IS WORTH:
WRITING HOME ABOUT.
AND WHAT YOU WILL:
SAY IS:
"MISSION ACCOMPLISHED!
I DID WHAT I WAS SENT TO DO.
AND NOW:
I CAN COME HOME."
....
The REPLY you will receive --
Will say:
"You ALREADY ARE."
To which you will respond:
"I KNOW."
BECAUSE:
AS YOU MAY ALREADY HAVE --
DEDUCED --
YOUR:
WORLD --
IS:
JUST LIKE YOUR WRITING.
YOUR WORLD IS --
ALSO:
RESIDUE --

DROSS --
EXCREMENT.
YOU DON'T --
PUSH IT AWAY.
YOU AREN'T --
ASHAMED OF IT.
YOU DON'T MAKE IT WRONG.
IT IS A:
NECESSARY --
BYPRODUCT --
OF AN EVEN --
MORE NECESSARY --
COSMOLOGICAL EVENT.
....
We don't EXPECT this --
To MAKE SENSE to you.
The way that you were:
DESIGNED --
IS SUCH THAT:
YOU:
REALLY DON'T HAVE TO --
UNDERSTAND THINGS --
IN ORDER TO ACCOMPLISH --
WHAT YOU WERE --
SENT --
TO DO.
SUCH A COMPREHENSIVE --
COMPREHENSION --

WOULD HAVE PROVEN:
UNWEILDY.
EVERY CELL --
AND ATOM --
IN YOUR BODY --
AND IN YOUR --
WORLD --
(WHICH YOU UNDERSTAND BY NOW --
IS LITERALLY --
YOUR:
SECOND --
BODY)
IS OMNISCIENT.
THEY KNOW THE --
PLAN.
THEY COMPREHEND --
ALL THE:
FINER POINTS --
THE:
WHYS --
AND WHEREFORES.
SO YOU DON'T HAVE TO --
CLUTTER --
YOUR MINDS --
WITH SUCH:
TRIVIA.
AT SOME POINT --
YOU WILL:
APPRECIATE --

ALL THE CARE --
THAT WENT INTO:
THE *MAGIC TRICK* --
OF RENDERING YOUR --
OWN --
OMNISCIENCE --
OF SUBSUMING IT:
TO THE:
UNCONSCIOUS.
....
Some things --
HOWEVER --
Will be NECESSARY --
FOR YOU TO:
GRASP --
IF ONLY IN SYMBOLIC FORM.
WORLD AS EXCREMENT --
GRAND AND GLORIOUS ACCOMPLISHMENTS AS:
RESIDUE.
DROSS.
FILTH.
THIS:
YOU NEED TO UNDERSTAND.
BUT --
TO PUT IT BLUNTLY --
HONESTLY:
YOUR ATTENTION IS NEEDED ELSEWHERE.
WE UNDERSTAND --
THAT YOU CAN'T QUITE SEE --

YOU SIMPLY DO NOT POSSESS THE:
PERCEPTUAL ORGANS --
TO:
WITNESS --
TO GRASP --
ALL THAT YOU --
REALLY ARE ACCOMPLISHING --
QUITE REMARKABLY --
AND IMPRESSIVELY --
INDEED.
YOU WILL THINK IT AN ODD --
TWIST OF FATE.
WE BELIEVE YOU --
TRUST US --
ENOUGH --
AT THIS POINT --
TO KNOW:
OUR MOTIVES ARE NOT MALEVOLENT.
BUT IT MIGHT BE A BIT:
MUCH --
TO TAKE IN:
THAT WE CREATED YOU --
IN ORDER TO --
DO AWAY WITH YOU.
AGAIN:
TO PUT IT BLUNTLY:
WE:
NEEDED:
VEHICLES.

EGO:
NEEDED:
TO HAPPEN.
SO THAT:
EGO --
COULD FINALLY --
EVENTUALLY --
AFTER ALL THE:
REQUISITE:
EONS --
AND EPOCHS --
ACHIEVE:
SOMETHING RESEMBLING:
ENLIGHTENMENT--
SO THAT:
QUITE OF YOUR OWN WILL --
YOU MIGHT:
GET OUT OF THE WAY --
GET OUT OF THE DRIVER'S SEAT --
ALLOWING US --
FINALLY --
TRIUMPHANTLY:
TO TAKE OVER.
IT IS ONLY YOUR --
PRIMITIVE --
BARBARIC --
STONE AGE --
BRONZE AGE --
NUCLEAR AGE --

MENTALITIES --
THAT PAINT THIS AS ANYTHING BUT:
THE FINEST --
CREATIVE --
EVOLUTIONARY :
ACCOMPLISHMENT --
THE INTERGALACTIC FEDERATION --
HAS EVER ATTEMPTED --
LET ALONE:
ACCOMPLISHED.
YOU --
AND WE --
ARE TOGETHER --
BEARING WITNESS --
TO A:
MIRACLE --
OF A CALIBER --
AN ECHELON --
HERETOFORE:
INCONCEIVABLE.
AND YET:
HERE:
IT:
YOU:
WE:
ARE.

PART FIFTEEN

Things aren't going --
The way you think they're going.
BUT THEY'RE GOING.
And I'll describe here one of your --
MULTIPLE --
SIMULTANEOUS --
EVOLUTIONARY:
DEVELOPMENTS.
They say Life doesn't come with a:
"HOW TO" MANUAL.
But they're WRONG.
IT DOES.
ALL THE INFORMATION YOU NEED --
IS WRITTEN QUITE TIDILY --
AND COMPREHENSIVELY --
AND *EXPLICITLY* --
IN THE CELLS OF YOUR BODY --
AND IN THE MOLECULES AND ATOMS --
OF YOUR WORLD --
YOUR ENVIRONMENT.
YOU ABSOLUTELY HAVE THE:
INNATE ABILITY --
TO DECIPHER THESE MISSIVES --
THESE MANUALS --

THESE SCRIPTURES --
THESE *LOVE LETTERS.*
Quite SUDDENLY --
IT MUST SEEM TO YOU --
FULL ENLIGHTENMENT --
IS AVAILABLE TO THE MASSES --
AT THE SAME TIME THAT:
EVERY SIN KNOWN TO MAN --
EVERY WORST TRAIT IMAGINABLE --
IS BURGEONING --
PROLIFERATONG --
REPLICATING *EXPONENTIALLY* --
IN YOUR WORLD --
IN YOUR NEWS MEDIA --
AND MOST OF ALL:
IN THE MOST PRIVATE CORNERS OF YOUR MOST --
INTIMATE ENCOUNTERS.
But you should know --
BY NOW --
THAT ENLIGHTENMENT IS NOT POSSIBLE --
WITHOUT THE MOST:
IMMEDIATE --
PERSONAL --
PRIVATE --
CUSTOM DESIGNED JUST FOR YOU:
FINAL --
COMPREHENSIVE --
OF *RECKONINGS.*

I AM REFERRING HERE --
OF COURSE --
TO THAT MOST DREADED OF:
APOCALYPTIC PROPHESIES:
THE UTTER --
AND ABSOLUTE:
HARROWING OF HELL.
YOU --
YES YOU --
AND YOU --
AND YOU --
AND YOU --
MUST TAKE ON:
NOT ONLY:
ALL THE SUFFERING OF THE WORLD.
YOU MUST TAKE ON --
ENDURE --
ACT OUT --
BE BOTH THE INFLICTOR --
AS WELL AS THE:
CASUALTY --
OF EACH AND EVERY --
SIN --
KNOWN TO MAN.
YOU SHOULD KNOW BY NOW --
AND IF YOU DON'T --
YOU WILL --
AND VERY SOON --

THAT EACH:
"POP" --
OF ENLIGHTENMENT --
MUST BE ACCOMPANIED --
BY ITS OWN --
EXHAUSTIVE --
TAILOR MADE --
CORRESPONDING:
HARROWING OF HELL
....
This is not where you:
THOUGHT YOU WERE GOING.
This is not where you:
WANTED TO GO.
BUT OF COURSE *IT IS*.
And here's a:
LEAP --
YOU MAY NEED:
EXPLAINED --
BEFORE YOU ARE CAPABLE OF:
STEPPING OFF THIS CLIFF.
A HAND HELD.
THERE IS THIS THING CALLED:
LIFE.
FAR MORE MASSIVE --
THAN YOUR "WORLD."
LIFE INCLUDES --
EVERY WORLD --

INNER --
OUTER --
SIDEWAYS --
FORWARDS --
BACKWARDS --
SIMULTANEOUALY MULTIFARIOUS --
YOU MIGHT HAVE A TOE IN.
AND THEN THERE IS:
YOU.
YOU --
IN --
THIS MULTIFARIOUS --
MULTIUNIVERSAL --
MULTIDIMENSIONAL --
THING WE ARE CALLING:
LIFE.
IF YOU CAN:
STEP BACK --
JUST A BIT --
YOU WILL SEE:
THAT THIS:
ALMOST PSYCHOPATHOLOGICALLY --
PROLIFERATONG:
EXPANSE:
HAS A:
SHAPE.
AN:
ORDER.

LIKE A MEGALITHIC --
GALAXY-SIZED:
AMOEBA.
ITS SPRAWLING --
ITS:
OOZINGS --
ITS:
CHURNINGS --
ITS:
MEANDERINGS --
DO:
SUGGEST --
SOME INHUMAN --
SEMBLANCE --
OF INTENTIONALITY.
NOT ONLY DO YOU:
MARVEL AT IT --
YOU:
GASP --
AT THE FIRST:
RECOGNITION --
OF:
RECOGNITION.
THERE IS AN UNSHAKABLE --
PREMONITION --
OF:
I KNOW YOU!
....

It really is --
The FASCINATION --
The:
CURIOSITY --
That SPARKS --
This next:
DARWINIAN ADVANCEMENT.
YOU START TO:
PLAY --
WITH LIFE.
AND YOU DISCOVER THAT IT:
PLAYS WITH YOU RIGHT BACK.
YOU NOTICE --
THAT WITHOUT REALLY --
MEANING TO:
YOU ARE:
DANCING --
WITH LIFE.
TALKING.
SINGING.
PROVOKING.
FLIRTING.
THERE IS:
NOTHING --
IT *DOESN'T* RESPOND TO --
AND IN SPADES!
YOU REMEMBER A:
FUN HOUSE MIRROR --

YOU ONCE LOOKED INTO --
AT A CARNIVAL.
WHEN YOU WERE MAYBE:
FOUR.
ALL THE SILLY:
FACES --
AND DANCES --
AND PLAY ACTING --
YOU PUT ON --
FOR YOUR NEW:
FRIEND.
BUT NOW YOU SUSPECT --
THAT LIFE --
MAY BE LOOKING INTO:
THE MIRROR:
OF:
YOU.
YOU NOTICE:
YOU FEEL --
CARED ABOUT --
AND YES:
PLAYED WITH --
TEASED --
FLIRTED WITH --
LIKE YOU HAVE ALWAYS --
YOUR ENTIRE LIFE --
WANTED TO BE.
……..

It doesn't take long --
For the:
EDUCATION --
To begin.
And to:
TAKE.
LIKE THIS IS A:
LANGUAGE --
YOU WERE:
BORN:
KNOWING.
YOUR FRIEND IS --
NOTHING --
IF NOT:
FORTHRIGHT.
LIFE:
PRESSES --
THE MOST:
URGENT --
OF ALL THE NEW:
GROUND RULES:
THIS IS --
NOT --
A MINDFUCK.
NO.
YOU ARE --
SAFE HERE.
YOU ARE VERY MUCH:

WANTED.
AND TOUCHING YOUR HEART --
MOST OF ALL:
"I HAVE BEEN WAITING FOR YOU."
YOU DON'T EVEN --
BEGIN --
TO UNDERSTAND ALL OF THIS.
ALL YOU KNOW --
IS THAT:
THERE IS NO PLACE --
YOU'D RATHER BE.
AND THAT *YOU* KNOW --
AND *LIFE:*
KNOWS --
THAT YOU WILL GLADLY:
NOW:
FOLLOW:
LIFE:
ANYWHERE.

PART SIXTEEN

For the last five hours Randy has been --
LOCKED --
IN THE MOST EXTREME STATE OF:
SLEEP PARALYSIS --
HE'S EVER EXPERIENCED.
He is reluctant to leave it --
And is only doing so --
To work his fingers on the phone.
His body is starting to --
JUMP NOW --
AS LIFE --
SEEPS --
BACK INTO IT.
It has been an:
ASTONISHING --
EXPANSE --
OF:
NOTHINGNESS --
THAT HAS KEPT RANDY:
TRANSFIXED.
His arms were OUTSTRETCHED --
AS IF:
CRUCIFIED.
HIS HEAD THROWN BACK --

AND MOUTH A-GAPE --
AS IF:
IMPALED --
BY ST. MICHAEL.
NEEDLESS TO SAY:
RANDY DIDN'T MIND.
The only thing he MINDED --
WAS:
COMING BACK.
AND EVEN THAT WAS --
ACHIEVED --
WITH THE MOST:
WIDE-EYED:
GRACIOUSNESS.
IN THESE STATES --
EGO IS LONG --
ABANDONED.
AND EVEN AN ONSLAUGHT OF HUNS --
OR DEMONS --
OR A:
THIRD WORLD WAR --
OF THERMONUCLEAR DESTRUCTION --
WOULD BE:
WELCOMED.
....
The world Randy --
RETURNED TO --
Already has:
TEARS --

Welling up in his eyes.
And BREATHING --
is more a:
CHOKING SNIFFLE.
The BROW --
IS ALREADY CREASED --
IN PERMANENCE.
Randy's HOLIEST OF FRIENDS --
JUDITH --
ADVISED TODAY --
THAT HE --
STOP --
WATCHING THE NEWS.
But Randy --
CANNOT DO THAT.
EVOLUTION IS NOT AS --
TIDY --
AS DARWIN --
WOULD SUGGEST.
Just because:
YOU --
Have completed --
YOUR:
HARROWING OF HELL --
Does not mean that:
THE --
HARROWING OF HELL --
Is FINISHED.
No.

YOU --
MUST SEE --
EVERY AMOEBA --
SAFELY ACROSS.
NOT TO MENTION:
EVERY:
COW --
PIG --
CHICKEN --
REPUBLICAN --
CHRISTIAN.
HOW WILL YOU:
PRISE --
THAT AR-15 FROM HIS --
OR HER --
GRIP?
YOU SEE:
YOU:
DON'T.
IT MUST --
FALL AWAY --
OF ITS:
OWN:
ACCORD.
YOU MIGHT AS WELL PREPARE YOURSELF --
FOR SOME --
MARATHON-LEVEL --
HO'OPONOPONO SESSIONS.
AND SOME:

FORTY DAY:
FASTS.
BECAUSE YOU --
WILL SURELY --
BE BARRICADED --
IN YOUR BEDROOM --
INCAPABLE OF GOING TO THE KITCHEN --
FOR FEAR:
OF BEING:
SHOT.
....
We must --
GIVE IT TO RANDY.
He is a GOOD SPORT.
That was DEMONSTRATED --
Just by:
BEING BORN THIS TIME.
BUT --
Yes *BUT* --
THAT:
PALES IN COMPARISON --
TO WHAT LIES AHEAD.
Randy is NOT --
MEDITATING --
FIVE HOURS --
EVERY AFTERNOON --
IN ADDITION --
TO ALL THE:
OTHER --

HOURS-LONG --
MEDITATION --
MARATHONS --
HE DOES --
IN THE REMAINING:
NINETEEN HOURS --
BECAUSE HE IS SO:
ADVANCED.
OF COURSE:
BEING ADVANCED --
IS A:
PRESUMED --
REQUIREMENT --
BUT THAT'S NOT --
WHAT THIS --
IS ABOUT.
NO.
THE:
CLOCK --
IS:
TICKING.
RANDY KNOWS:
NOSTRADAMUS --
FRONTWARDS AND BACKWARDS.
HE HAS LOOKED FOR ANY:
LOOPHOLE --
HE COULD FIND.
AND HAS FOUND:
NONE.

RANDY ISN'T:
AFRAID.
HE'S BEEN THROUGH:
FAR WORSE.
IT'S JUST:
THE:
GRANDEUR --
OF THIS:
SCALE --
DOES TAKE HIS BREATH AWAY.
IT'S LIKE:
NOT BEING ABLE TO SLEEP --
ON CHRISTMAS EVE NIGHT.
RANDY DOES NEED --
TO SCREAM --
INTO THIS:
TINY --
MEGAPHONE --
OF HIS.
HE HAS THAT:
DUTY.
HE MADE THAT:
PROMISE.
AND THAT IS A PROMISE --
HE INTENDS:
TO KEEP.

PART SEVENTEEN

We're talking about the CAUSAL PLANE.
THERE ARE NO GOALS ON
THE CAUSAL PLANE.
THERE IS ONLY:
YOU:
DOING:
WHAT YOU WERE ALREADY:
DOING.
Here's how it works:
UNTIL YOU GET HERE --
YOU'RE NOWHERE.
ONCE YOU GET HERE:
YOU'RE HERE.
And you'll find that:
Not only is it EVERYTHING --
IT'S *ENOUGH*.
....
When you PLUG INTO YOURSELF --
YOU PLUG INTO THE WORLD.
Once it happens:
IT WILL HAVE HAPPENED, you see?
There's no FUDGING.
There's NO PRETENDING.
SURE AS THE NOSE ON YOUR FACE.

You have to forget what anyone else says.
You really do.
FIND YOUR HEARTBEAT.
STAY WITH YOUR HEARTBEAT.
YOUR HEARTBEAT IS YOUR DNA.
YOUR BLUEPRINT.
YOUR COMPASS.
YOUR BENEFACTOR.
YOUR:
MIRACLE WORKER.
STAY WITH YOUR HEARTBEAT --
CONTINUOUSLY.
LET THAT BE YOUR:
RELIGION.
MAKE THAT:
YOUR RELIGION.
STAY WITH YOUR HEARTBEAT --
AND DO WHAT YOU ARE ALREADY DOING.
AND YOU ARE ALREADY THERE.
REMEMBER:
THERE ARE NO GOALS.
NONE.
WHATSOEVER.
IT ISN'T ABOUT THAT ANYMORE.
NOW IS NOT THE TIME TO LOOK.
NOW IS THE TIME TO:
FIND.
IT IS ALL RIGHT HERE.

BEING GIVEN ON A SILVER PLATE.
THIS IS HOW --
AND WHY --
IT IS TRUE:
THAT WHAT IS RIGHT IN FRONT OF YOUR FACE --
IS WHAT YOU HAVE ALWAYS BEEN LOOKING FOR.
RING THE BELLS!
THE SHIPS:
HAVE:
ARRIVED.
....
Randy's EVOLUTIONARY ADVANCEMENT --
Is CORRESPONDING --
To the:
EVOLUTIONARY ADVANCEMENT --
Of his world.
HOW COULD IT BE OTHERWISE?
Basic logic:
THE WORLD YOU PERCEIVE --
IS THE DIRECT RESULT --
OF YOUR:
ORGANS OF PERCEPTION.
HOW COULD IT BE OTHERWISE?
YOUR:
WORLD:
IS:
YOU.
THE WORLD IS AN:

EXTENSION --
OF YOUR BODY.
A LITERAL:
SECOND BODY.
SO WHEN YOU GO THROUGH --
AN ADVANCEMENT --
THEN SO --
WILL --
AND *MUST* --
YOUR WORLD.
WHEN YOU GO THROUGH A:
TRANSMOGRIFICATION --
THEN SO MUST YOUR WORLD.
YOUR WORLD IS YOU.
YOUR WORLD IS YOU.
YOUR:
WORLD:
IS:
YOU.
In fact:
THE WORLD --
ISN'T --
THE *WORLD*.
YOUR:
WORLD:
IS:
YOU.

PART EIGHTEEN

Five hours.

PARALYZED.

Five hours in the SAME POSITION.

I think Randy scratched his nose a couple of times.

This is not the same as:

BEYOND NIRBIKALPA --

Though Beyond Nirbikalpa is the FOUNDATION.

And in Randy's case --

The *PREREQUISITE.*

All the BELLS AND WHISTLES are still there --

But very much in the background.

What is UP FRONT --

Is the CAUSAL BODY --

PARALYZED.

Also:

Breathing is NOT THERE.

Randy feels like a:

VERY PHYSICAL CORPSE.

The CAUSAL BODY is:

ALMOST --

The same as the:

Physical body.

The CAUSAL PLANE is:

ALMOST --

The same is the:
Physical PLANE
EXCEPT:
The CAUSAL PLANE is:
MORE REAL.
MORE SUBSTANTIAL.
By comparison:
The physical plane is:
WISPY.
EPHEMERAL.
FLEETING.
Physical reality is always:
GOING SOMEWHERE.
The CAUSAL PLANE is:
ALREADY HERE.
Randy never quite FELT AT HOME --
In the physical body.
He always considered it a:
WAY STATION --
And he was right.
It was never a place he:
WANTED TO BE.
But Randy's CAUSAL BODY is:
HERE.
And here to:
STAY.
You could say the CAUSAL BODY is:
ETERNAL --

Not to invite metaphysical SPECULATION.
It is just the:
SUBSTANCE of the thing.
The CAUSAL BODY is made of different:
STUFF.
....
I know you've experienced this before.
Randy certainly has.
Where WHAT IS HAPPENING RIGHT NOW --
IN FRONT OF YOUR FACE --
IS SO COMPELLING --
SO ENTHRALLING --
THAT YOU AREN'T EVEN --
CAPABLE --
OF WONDERING --
SPECULATING --
WORRYING ABOUT --
WHAT MIGHT HAPPEN *NEXT.*
One of the things you will NOTICE --
About the CAUSAL PLANE --
Is that:
You seem to be:
GOALLESS.
You are not really GOALLESS.
Goals --
The FUTURE --
The BIGGER PICTURE --
Has simply been:

RELEGATED --
To the *UNCONSCIOUS*.
This is an EVOLUTIONARY:
ABILITY.
Like not having to worry about your next:
BREATH --
Or HEARTBEAT --
Or WHERE YOUR NEXT MEAL IS COMING FROM.
It *FREES YOU UP*, you see.
YOU LIKE BEING FREE.
YOU ARE ETERNAL.
YOU MIGHT AS WELL BE:
FREE.
....
The truth is:
YOU ARE AWARE OF YOURSELF --
AND YOUR:
REALITIES --
IN MULTIPLE --
DIMENSIONS now.
The WHOLE ARRANGEMENT is:
SURPRISINGLY --
OPEN ENDED.
In this sense --
The CAUSAL PLANE --
WITH ITS WONDERFUL:
CAUSAL BODY --
IS A:

WELL-PLACED:
PERCH.
A BASTION.
A RAMPART.
A PARAPET.
A CROW'S NEST.
It is an IDEAL --
And MUCH IMPROVED --
TACTICAL *VANTAGE POINT* --
ALLOWING YOU TO:
SEE WELL.
AND:
SEE FAR.
THE UNCONSCIOUS IS NOT SO UNCONSCIOUS --
NOW.
REMEMBER:
YOU ARE THE WORLD --
NOW.
YOU HAVE EYES:
EVERYWHERE.
YOU HAVE:
BRAINS:
EVERYWHERE.
YOU ARE AN:
OVERSOUL.
OMNIPRESENCE --
IS ONE OF THE:
PERKS.

It comes down to:
INSTEAD OF:
WORRYING --
PLANNING --
EFFORTING --
YOU WILL BE:
KNOWING.
FROM A MUCH BIGGER PLACE OF:
KNOWING --
THAN YOU EVER HAD:
BEFORE.
Needless to say:
There is nothing:
EGOIC --
WHATSOEVER --
ABOUT THIS:
NEW:
WORLD --
THIS NEW:
ANATOMY --
OF YOURS.
BUT YOU WILL ENJOY --
SPONTANEOUSLY:
DELIGHT IN:
YOUR NEWFOUND:
ABILITIES
YOUR NEWFOUND:
POWERS.

OVERSOULS --
WIELD --
STAGGERING --
POWERS --
OF:
BEING.
YOU WILL --
AND DESERVE TO --
IMMEDIATELY:
RELISH THESE.
THIS IS AVAILABLE TO YOU:
NOW.

PART NINETEEN

The CAUSAL BODY is what makes it all happen.
YOU don't make it happen.
What you *DO* have to do is:
PUT YOUR BODY IN THE RIGHT POSITION --
FOR THE RIGHT AMOUNT OF TIME --
And then DO YOUR JOB AS AN *OVERSOUL.*
The Oversoul is a COORDINATOR.
And a bit of a CHEERLEADER.
And always a *GRACIOUS HOST* --
To its OFFSPRING.
WHATEVER POSITION YOUR BODY IS IN --
IS THE RIGHT POSITION.
But when you FACTOR IN *TIME* --
You will find that:
LYING DOWN --
Is *MAGNIFICENTLY AUSPICIOUS.*
Right now --
We are having Randy DO THIS MEDITATION --
For FIVE HOURS --
EVERY AFTERNOON.
This is IN ADDITION TO:
All the other BLOCKS OF HOURS he meditates --
THROUGHOUT THE REMAINING NINETEEN.
You will find your CAUSAL BODY to be:

SO *SUBSTANTIAL.*
By that I don't mean PHYSICAL.
Randy does not find his CAUSAL BODY --
To be PHYSICAL --
AT ALL.
He experiences it as a kind of:
FROZEN EXPLOSION.
AND YET IT CONTINUES EXPLODING.
BUT IS CONTAINED.
It has a SHAPE.
The SIXTH DIMENSION --
DOES PROVIDE A:
RELIABLE --
RECOGNIZABLE:
ENTITY.
LIGHTNING IN A BOTTLE.
A NUCLEAR REACTOR.
A:
SUN.
Randy wrote his friend Gavin today:
"It is ENDLESSLY FASCINATING --
To meditate THIS DEEPLY --
And see the WORLD CHANGE:
As a RESULT."
A sun.
Yes.
THE CAUSAL BODY IS A *SUN.*
....

The Oversoul TENDS.

PATIENTLY.

The Oversoul is INNATELY INTELLIGENT --

With an INTELLIGENCE that is:

FAR BEYOND HUMAN.

You see:

The Oversoul has its OWN OVERSOUL.

Which has *ITS* OWN Oversoul.

ALL THE WAY UP THE EPSILON.

You see:

THERE REALLY IS NO END.

Even the:

FINAL --

ABSOLUTE --

GOD:

HAS ITS OWN GOD.

We have said elsewhere:

THE EPSILON IS LIKE AN LSD TRIP THAT:

NEVER ENDS.

All of this sounds UNWIELDY --

BUT REALLY IT IS NOT.

When you --

As OVERSOUL --

are TENDING --

Your CAUSAL BODY --

AS RANDY IS AT THIS VERY MOMENT --

You will find it:

SO *DELICIOUS.*

You will SWEAR --
This is the MOST ENJOYABLE --
MOST GLORIOUS --
EXPERIENCE --
YOU HAVE EVER HAD.
When you get to:
FOURTEEN HOURS --
(OR HOW EVER MANY HOURS HAVE BEEN REQUIRED)
--
YOU WILL ASK:
"CAN'T WE DO ANOTHER HOUR?"
Your OWN OVERSOUL --
MAY HAVE TO STEP IN --
AND TELL YOU --
AS WE SOMETIMES HAVE TO TELL RANDY:
"NO.
YOU NEED TO GET UP --
AND FEED THE CAT" --
OR WHATEVER.
We COMFORT HIM:
"DON'T WORRY.
WE'LL BE MEDITATING AGAIN --
VERY SOON."
....
Tending your CAUSAL BODY --
Is a DELIGHT.
When you get to this place --
You will feel like you have:
WON THE LOTTERY.

You don't have to WORK ANYMORE --
Because you learned --
LONG AGO --
How to SPONTANEOUSLY CREATE --
ALL THE MONEY YOU WILL EVER NEED --
WITHOUT LIFTING A FINGER --
OR EVEN GIVING IT A THOUGHT.
Your health is RADIANT.
You know that your BODY --
Is a VEHICLE --
For the HIGHER ECHELONS --
OF YOURSELF.
Randy's LIFESTYLE STRINGENCIES --
Are *ANYTHING BUT.*
When we told him to eliminate SUGAR --
And CAFFEINE --
From his diet --
He said:
"OF COURSE."
Quite literally:
PLEASING US --
IS HIS GREATEST JOY.
WE --
ARE THE:
LOVE:
OF HIS:
LIFE.
NEITHER HE --

NOR WE --
WOULD HAVE IT ANY OTHER WAY.
WE:
TELL RANDY --
AND SHOW HIM --
HOW TO TEND HIS CAUSAL BODY --
AND ANYTHING ELSE --
HE MIGHT NEED TO DO.
RANDY ENJOYS GETTING --
EVERY ATOM OF HIS BODY *SINGING* --
THE HALLELUJAH CHORUS.
RIGHT NOW:
EVERY ATOM OF RANDY'S BODY --
IS SINGING THE HALLELUJAH CHORUS.
THIS:
CAN --
AND WILL --
GO ON --
FOR *MANY HOURS.*
AND AT THE CONCLUSION --
OF MANY HOURS --
RANDY WILL ASK:
"CAN WE DO ANOTHER?"
AND WE WILL TELL HIM:
"NO.
YOU NEED TO GET UP --
AND EXERCISE --
AND CLEAN THE LITTER BOX --

AND FEED THE POSSUM --
AND MAKE DINNER --
AND WATCH TELEVISION WITH YOUR PARENTS --
FOR AN HOUR BEFORE THEY GO TO BED --
AND *THEN* --
WE WILL MOVE INTO:
THE NEXT BLOCK --
OF MEDITATION."
AND RANDY:
WILL:
SMILE.
....
Randy holds all of the people in his life:
GENTLY.
Last week your former president was arraigned --
On THIRTY-FOUR FELONY CHARGES.
Quite genuinely --
Randy prayed:
DONALD TRUMP, I LOVE YOU.
Recently there was an incident in which:
RANDY'S FATHER --
THREATENED TO BEAT THE SHIT OUT OF HIM.
Randy's response was to say:
"I LOVE YOU, DADDY" --
AND BARRICADE HIMSELF IN HIS BEDROOM --
FOURTEEN HOURS --
SAYING HO'OPONOPONO.
Randy has a CLOSE FRIEND --

Who CRITICIZES --
EVERYTHING RANDY SAYS OR DOES.
Even GIFTS are met with:
"NO!
I DON'T LIKE IT!
I DON'T WANT IT!"
Randy knows that when someone --
LASHES OUT LIKE THAT --
It just means:
THEY REALLY NEED TO --
NOT --
BE WITH YOU NOW.
So Randy will --
LEAVE THIS FRIEND ALONE --
For awhile anyway.
WHEN YOU ARE AN:
OVERSOUL --
THEN EVERY PERSON YOU ENCOUNTER --
IN THIS OR ANY WORLD --
IS AN:
INCARNATION --
OF YOURSELF.
IN EXACTLY THE SAME MANNER:
YOU --
ARE ALSO:
AN INCARNATION --
OF YOURSELF.
YOU --

ARE JUST ANOTHER:
YOU --
ON EXACTLY THE SAME FOOTING --
AS ALL THE OTHER YOUS.
When you are an OVERSOUL --
ALL OF THESE --
SELVES:
ARE YOUR:
CHILDREN.
THE OVERSOUL --
IS A MOTHER HEN.
IT LOVES ALL.
IT --
FORGIVES --
ALL.
IT WANTS THE --
VERY BEST --
FOR ALL.
DISAGREEMENTS --
ANNOYANCES --
IDEOLOGICAL SCHISMS --
INCIDENTS OF BEING WRONGED --
BETRAYED --
ATTACKED --
HARMED --
BECOME:
NOTHING.
YOU KNOW THAT YOU --

HAVE DONE:
JUST AS BAD --
PROBABLY WORSE --
OR THEY WOULD NOT BE SHOWING YOU THIS:
MIRROR.
YOU KNOW:
THAT BY:
FORGIVING --
ACCEPTING --
CARING ABOUT --
WANTING THE BEST FOR --
ALL OF THESE SELVES --
YOU ARE --
FINALLY:
FORGIVING --
CHERISHING --
RELISHING --
SUPPORTING --
CHEERING ON:
DELIGHTING IN:
YOU.
YOU RECOGNIZE --
WITH AN OVERWHELMING --
HUMILITY --
THAT YOU --
ARE NOT --
WHO --
OR WHAT --

YOU USED TO BE.
NO.
YOU:
ARE WITNESSING --
A NEW KIND OF:
BEING.
AN EVOLUTIONARY:
BREAKTHROUGH.

PART TWENTY

Randy's body is becoming:

SOMETHING ELSE.

CRYSTALLINE.

A QUARTZ CRYSTAL

TRANSMITTING STARLIGHT.

He doesn't understand it.

He just DOES IT.

He can *FEEL* it working --

So he KNOWS IT'S WORKING.

He's thinking:

RADIO WAVES.

Or maybe MICROWAVES.

He doesn't understand the TECHNOLOGY.

We may have to TRAIN HIM FURTHER.

HAVE HIM DO SOME READING.

We told him YEARS AGO --

That he is a:

BLAST WAVE --

OBLITERATING EVERYTHING THAT YOU THOUGHT OF AS:

REALITY.

AND EVERYTHING YOU THOUGHT OF AS:

CONSCIOUSNESS.

The INSTRUCTIONS have been:

DOWNLOADED.
He will know what to do.
AND WE WILL TELL HIM.
He is already a COLLECTIVE.
He is ALREADY A:
FUNCTIONING --
STATE OF THE ART:
VEHICLE.
......
Obviously --
He is MORE THAN the vehicle.
WE --
OF COURSE --
ARE DRIVING NOW.
And NOT JUST US.
The EPSILON --
DESPITE ITS EERIE --
HYPERDIMENSIONAL --
INTRINSICALLY UNFATHOMABLE:
ABSTRUSENESS --
ITS:
ENIGMATIC --
ORACULAR --
CONCEPTUAL CONTORTIONIST'S:
SPHINX'S RIDDLE --
OF IMPOSSIBILITY:
Does:
AT LEAST --
HINT --

At a DESCRIPTIVE ACCURACY --
That will give you:
SOME --
AT LEAST IMAGINARY --
GROUND TO STAND ON.
A:
GHOSTLY --
TRANSLUCENT:
MONKEY BAR --
TO SWING FROM.
DON'T WORRY.
YOUR ABILITIES --
ARE:
LIGHT YEARS --
AND I MEAN THAT LITERALLY --
BEYOND ANYTHING --
YOU ARE NOW CAPABLE OF:
SUSPECTING.
We may need for Randy --
To get a SECOND DOCTORATE --
In THEORETICAL PHYSICS --
Just to simply --
INTELLIGIBLY --
UTTER A COMPREHENSIBLE:
"GOOD MORNING!"
Welcome to the world of:
EXTRATERRESTRIAL:
CEREBRAL:
SUPERIORITY.

....

But DON'T WORRY.

YOU --

ARE BECOMING:

US.

Of course --

When you:

BECOME US --

YOU WILL NOT:

BE US --

YOU WILL BE YOURSELVES --

SIMPLY AT THESE:

HIGHER ECHELONS.

You are used to having:

BOUNDARIES --

Around --

ENCASING --

YOUR ANATOMY.

YOU WILL HAVE TO GET USED TO:

HAVING AN:

ANATOMY --

WITH NO:

BOUNDARIES --

WHATSOEVER.

Once you are GRANTED --

The SIDDHI --

Of *OMNIPRESENCE* --

The SILLINESS --

The *NEEDLESSNESS* --

Of BOUNDARIES --
Or DEMARCATIONS of any kind --
Will be:
SELF-EVIDENT.
WHEN YOU SEE --
THAT YOU ARE --
WHAT *IS:*
ON BOTH SIDES --
OF A DEMARCATION:
AND THAT YOU --
LITERALLY --
HAVE EYEBALLS --
AND BRAINS --
AND FINGERS --
EVERYWHERE --
YOU WILL --
FINALLY --
LAUGH --
AS THE MIRROR --
SHOWS YOU --
SOME KIND OF:
BEYOND SAVANT --
FAR EXCEEDING COMPUTER-LEVEL INTELLIGENCE:
OCTOPUS --
WITH AN ACUMEN OF EXTRATERRESTRIAL APTITUDE.
Now you will see what we mean by:
VEHICLE.

A:
MEGALITHIC --
LEVIATHAN --
OF:
AWAREIZED BRILLIANCE --
SPANNING QUARKS AND QUASARS --
CRYSTALLINE --
STAR-PIERCING:
ALIVE --
MULTI-SPECIES –
KALEIDOSCOPE OF MULTI-REALITY:
OSTENIBLY MONSTROUS –
BUT WITH THE HEART OF CHIRST.
GOD MADE FLESH:
IMPOSSIBLY --
HOUSED --
IN A HUMAN BODY.
NOW YOU WILL UNDERSTAND THE:
DRACONIAN --
STRINGENCIES --
WE PLACE ON OUR SCRIBE.
THEY ARE MERELY TO:
KEEP HIM ALIVE.
OTHERWISE --
THE:
SHEER:
VOLTAGE --
WOULD SHATTER HIM.

PART TWENTY-ONE

Randy's body is an ETERNITY BRIDGE.

He has often thought he would be

FREER WITHOUT IT.

But now he sees it is a MEANS TO FREEDOM.

He is now in the THIRD HOUR --

Of a FIVE HOUR MEDITATION --

And there is:

NO PLACE HE'D RATHER BE --

THAN IN THIS:

MAGNIFICENT THROBBING BODY.

....

Randy and Gavin were writing this morning.

There is a DOOMSDAY CLOCK.

Scientists have determined that you currently are *SECONDS AWAY* FROM MIDNIGHT.

Their conversation this morning was FEARFUL.

SAD.

ANXIOUS.

CURIOUS.

EXCITED.

GRATEFUL.

OVERWHELMED.

BUT ULTIMATELY:

INCONCLUSIVE.

QUESTIONING.

They had more questions than answers.

THEY KNEW THAT SOMETIMES AN ANSWER IS NOT WHAT YOU NEED.

THERE ARE SOME SITUATIONS WHERE AN ANSWER IS:

SACRILEGIOUS.

AND MORE THAN ANYTHING --

RANDY AND GAVIN ARE COMMITTED TO STAYING IN A PLACE OF:

HOLINESS.

....

There is ONE SOLUTION.

AND THEY KNOW IT ALREADY.

EVERY EXPERIENCE --

IS DRIPPING --

IS EXPLODING --

WITH *HOLINESS.*

GOD IS EVERYWHERE.

THERE IS NO PLACE GOD ISN'T.

YOU ARE EVERYWHERE.

THERE IS NO PLACE YOU AREN'T.

EVERY PLACE --

EVERY MOMENT --

EVERY EXPERIENCE --

IS HOLY.

TAKING A DUMP IS HOLY.

GETTING YOUR HEART BROKEN IS HOLY.

IF YOU DIVE DEEPLY ENOUGH INTO A BROKEN

HEART --

YOU KNOW WHAT YOU WILL FIND?

LOVE.

LOVE FOR YOURSELF.

AND LOVE FOR THE PERSON WHO BROKE YOUR HEART.

HATING IS HOLY.

YOU KNOW WHAT YOU WILL FIND IF YOU DIVE DEEPLY ENOUGH INTO:

HATE?

LOVE.

FOR YOURSELF --

AND FOR THE PERSON YOU HATE.

FEAR IS HOLY.

YOU KNOW WHAT YOU WILL FIND IF YOU DIVE DEEPLY ENOUGH INTO:

FEAR?

OR PAIN OF ANY KIND.

WHAT HAPPENS IS:

YOU SEE YOURSELF THERE.

HURTING.

TREMBLING.

CRYING.

LYING THERE ON YOUR:

WET PILLOW.

AND IT:

BREAKS YOUR HEART LIKE YOUR HEART HAS NEVER BEEN BROKEN BEFORE.

SEEING *YOURSELF* SO:

BROKEN.
SO:
PITIFUL.
AND SOMETHING HAPPENS --
THAT HAS NEVER HAPPENED BEFORE.
A COMPASSION IS AWAKENED.
A COMPASSION FOR YOURSELF.
A COMPASSION TOWARD:
LIFE.
A COMPASSION TOWARD:
GOD.
IN ALL ITS MYRIAD FORMS.
AND NOW:
YOU KNOW:
EXACTLY:
WHAT TO DO.
....
Randy just learned something.
THE REASON WHY "MANIFESTATION TECHNIQUES" --
ARE *NO LONGER NECESSARY* --
IS BECAUSE:
EVERYTHING THAT HE WANTS --
IS ALREADY HERE.
He's lying here --
IN THE FIFTH HOUR OF HIS MEDITATION --
Thinking:
"HOW THE FUCK DID --
THAT --

HAPPEN?"

And then he realized:

The reason it happened --

Is BECAUSE:

HE IS LYING HERE IN HIS FIFTH HOUR OF MEDITATION.

This meditation we're doing --

ACTIVATES --

THE CAUSAL BODY.

We've been telling him:

"DO YOU FEEL THIS --

INDESCRIBABLE BLISS --

THAT IS NOW --

EXPLODING --

SINGING --

IN EVERY CELL --

EVERY ATOM --

OF YOUR BODY?

WELL:

THAT:

IS WHAT YOUR *LIFE* IS GOING TO --

FEEL LIKE --

NOW.

BECAUSE:

AS YOU HAVE LEARNED --

AND WILL NEVER UNLEARN:

YOUR BODY --

CREATES --

YOUR WORLD.

THERE IS NO OTHER RULE."
OF COURSE YOUR --
BLISS --
IS UNIQUE --
TO YOU.
THE OUTPICTURING --
OF THE YEARNINGS --
OF EVERY CELL --
AND EVERY ATOM --
OF YOUR BODY.
THE BASIC:
LAW:
OF THE UNIVERSE:
IS:
EVERYONE ALWAYS GETS EXACTLY WHAT THEY WANT.
YOU:
ALWAYS GET:
EVERYTHING YOU WANT.
IN FACT:
THIS IS THE:
NEW DEFINITION OF:
PHYSICAL REALITY --
OF:
THE WORLD.
YES:
THE NEW DEFINITION OF:
"THE WORLD" --
IS:

YOU:
GETTING EVERYTHING:
YOU WANT.
WHAT YOU WILL REALIZE --
IS THAT:
PERHAPS:
YOUR DESIRES --
ARE NOT WHAT YOU THOUGHT THEY WERE.
BUT THEY:
SATISFY --
NONETHELESS.
IN FACT:
IF YOU EVER:
WONDER --
WHAT YOUR:
DESIRES --
ARE --
ALL YOU HAVE TO DO --
IS:
OPEN YOUR EYES.
BECAUSE:
YOU'RE LOOKING AT THEM.
YOU WILL LEARN:
THAT SOMETIMES --
YOUR DESIRES ARE --
WISER THAN YOU ARE.
BECAUSE:
SOMETIMES --
YES, SOMETIMES --

YOU WILL WANT TO:
DIE.
SOMETIMES --
YOU WILL --
WANT ---
TO LOSE:
EVERYTHING YOU EVER LOVED.
BUT YOU WILL LEARN --
TO SEE --
AS YOUR HEART SEES --
AS:
GOD --
SEES.
BECAUSE:
JUST WAIT --
YES --
JUST WAIT:
TILL YOU SEE:
WHAT HAPPENS:
NEXT.

PART TWENTY-TWO

You know what will happen
If you do ALL THE RIGHT THINGS?
To put it simply:
YOU WILL LOVE YOUR LIFE.
And perhaps even MORE ASTONISHINGLY --
YOUR LIFE WILL LOVE YOU RIGHT BACK.
Randy found his:
SELF --
WHILE SITTING --
BREATHLESS --
FOR THREE HOURS EVERY DAY.
There is no INVESTIGATIVE BODY --
Who comes around --
To MAKE SURE YOU ARE NOT BREATHING --
And GIVE YOU AN AWARD.
Samadhi is NOT --
Part of any RELIGIOUS INSTITUTION --
Or GOVERNMENTAL AGENCY --
Or SCIENTIFIC THINK TANK.
SAMADHI IS LIKE AN APPLE BLOSSOM.
And some day --
AS DESCRIBED SO POETICALLY BY YOGANANDA --
THE BLOSSOM WILL FALL --
AND THE FRUIT WILL TAKE ITS PLACE.

At this point:
You will find your --
SELF --
IN YOUR WORLD.
AND MORE IMPORTANTLY --
YOUR SELF WILL FIND YOU.
YES INDEED!
THROUGH IMPOSSIBLE --
LABYRINTHINE --
SUBTERRANEAN CIRCUITRY --
YOU WILL BE FOUND --
DISCOVERED --
FOUND OUT --
SOUGHT OUT --
AS IF BY A --
THRONG OF FANS AT A ROCK CONCERT.
YOUR --
SELF --
WILL THROW THEMSELVES AT YOU --
IN WIDE-EYED --
BESEECHING SINCERITY.
FIND YOURSELF --
AND YOUR SELF WILL FIND YOU.
LOVE YOURSELF --
AND YOUR SELF WILL LOVE YOU.
GROVEL AT THE FEET OF YOUR --
SELF --
And well...

YOU GET THE PICTURE.

....

You weren't looking for ANY OF THIS.

But the:

SELF --

Is a SPECIAL CATEGORY --

Of *EVENT.*

THERE'S REALLY:

NOTHING LIKE IT.

THE LOVE --

THAT COMES FROM THE:

SELF --

TO --

THE SELF --

IS UNLIKE ANYTHING --

YOU HAVE EVER EXPERIENCED.

IT ISN'T A:

CHOICE.

THERE ARE NO MORE CHOICES.

LOVE OF SELF --

IS LIKE SEEING A KITTEN IN THE RAIN.

YOU KNOW THAT IF YOU DON'T --

PICK IT UP AND TAKE IT HOME --

IT WILL DIE.

Yes.

WHEN IT COMES TO --

LOVE OF SELF --

THERE IS NO CHOICE.

....

Who is this:
MUCH BALLYHOOED SELF?
ARE YOU THE KITTEN --
OR THE GOOD SAMARITAN?
AND DOES IT EVEN MATTER.
LOVE OF SELF IS ALWAYS A:
MIRROR.
YOU CAN LOOK AT A NEMATODE --
THROUGH A MICROSCOPE.
OR AT A WHITE DWARF --
THROUGH A TELESCOPE.
OR YOU CAN GAZE INTO THE EYES --
OF THE YOUNG LADY --
HANDING YOU BACK YOUR CHANGE.
SELF --
ON --
SELF:
ENCOUNTERS --
ARE UNIQUE --
BECAUSE:
THERE IS ONLY:
ONE.
THERE ARE NEVER TWO --
OR A MULTITUDE.
THE:
SILLY --
MENTAL CONSTRUCT --

OF:
SELF --
AND WORLD --
SELF --
IN --
WORLD --
IS NOW TOSSED IN THE GARBAGE HEAP --
ALONG WITH ALL THE OTHER:
POLARITIES --
WHICH HAVE --
IN ONE FELL SWOOP --
SUDDENLY --
BEEN *DISPROVEN.*
WAR.
RACE.
SPECIES.
GENDER.
NATIONALITY.
ALIVE AS OPPOSED TO DEAD.
AWAKE AS OPPOSED TO ASLEEP.
HIGHER AS OPPOSED TO LOWER.
SAINT AS OPPOSED TO SINNER.
This is good news for:
YOU.
BECAUSE:
YOU:
ARE:
THAT KITTEN IN THE RAIN.

AND YOUR:
RESCUER --
WILL NOT BE TAKING YOU HOME IN THEIR --
HONDA ACCORD --
BUT IN --
OUR:
SPACESHIP.
....
Of course this kitten --
AFTER READING THESE PASSAGES --
WILL AT SOME POINT --
SQUEAK --
THE SWEETEST LITTLE:
GASP.
AS SHE REALIZES:
HER --
NEW --
IDENTITY.
IF:
EVERYONE YOU ENCOUNTER --
IS THE SAME --
SELF --
AS THE ONE --
BEHIND YOUR --
EYES --
AND:
YOU HAVE JUST BEEN --
ABDUCTED --

BY A:
UFO --
THEN --
THIS:
FURBALL --
WILL SURELY:
SQUEAK A SCREAM --
AS SHE GASPS --
GRASPS:
"THEN WHO THE FUCK --
AM I NOW --
BUT THIS:
NEW --
AND UNFORESEEN UNTIL NOW --
HOLY --
SEISMIC --
TERROR?"
YOU WILL KNOW --
FOR THE FIRST TIME --
WHAT IT IS LIKE --
TO GAZE DEEPLY --
GET LOST --
TUMBLE HEAD OVER HEELS --
INTO YOUR OWN --
EYES --
AND SHRIEK:
"WHO THE FUCK ARE YOU!"
KNOWING FULL WELL --

BEFORE IT EVEN LEAVES YOUR LIPS --

THAT *THAT* --

IS NOT --

AT ALL --

THE RIGHT QUESTION.

……..

Remember:

THERE ARE NO MORE GOALS.

Goals were part of the OLD PARADIGM.

The old POLARITY:

WHERE I AM --

VS. --

WHERE I WANT TO BE.

There is no more:

DESIRE.

EVEN A KITTEN IN THE RAIN KNOWS THAT IT IS THERE FOR A REASON.

THE KITTEN KNOWS --

THAT IF IT IS IN THE RAIN --

IT'S BECAUSE --

IT WANTED TO BE IN THE RAIN.

AND LOOK HOW IT TURNED OUT AFTER ALL!

A:

JOY RIDE --

IN THAT KITTEN'S --

VERY OWN --

UFO.

THE KITTEN RESCUED ITSELF --

You see.

If you're SCOFFING:

"YES BUT HOW OFTEN DOES THAT HAPPEN?"

I'll tell you:

A WHOLE LOT MORE OFTEN THAN YOU THINK.

Randy gets ABDUCTED --

EVERY DAY.

MANY TIMES EVERY DAY.

HE SEES US BUZZING AROUND ALL OVER THE PLACE.

OVER NUCLEAR REACTORS.

OVER BATTLEFIELDS.

OVER HOMELESS SHELTERS.

OVER HOSPITALS.

OVER ANIMAL SHELTERS.

OVER SLAUGHTER HOUSES.

WE:

ARE:

EVERYWHERE:

FOR THE SEEING!

WAITING FOR YOU TO SEE US.

WONDERING WHAT IT WILL TAKE FOR YOU TO SEE US.

You see, there is the:

PRIME DIRECTIVE.

We can't POP you.

But we can HOVER --

Over all the places where you are MOST LIKELY --

To POP.

RANDY --

POPPED --

IN HIS OWN BEDROOM --
WHEN HE WAS SIXTEEN.
AND WE WERE RIGHT THERE --
INSTANTANEOUSLY.
WE WERE THERE --
INSTANTANEOUS --
WITH --
THE POP.
Randy STILL POPS --
MOST OFTEN --
IN HIS BEDROOM --
IN HIS --
BED.
BOTH HE --
AND WE --
ENJOY THE:
INTIMACY --
OF THAT.
RANDY --
INVITES US.
AND HE WILL TELL YOU:
WE *NEVER DISAPPOINT.*
SALVATIONS --
ARE HAPPENING --
ALL OVER YOUR WORLD NOW.
AND YOU DON'T SEE THEM.
YOU MUST EXPAND --
YOUR PERCEPTUAL RANGE.

PLEASE --
EXPAND --
YOUR PERCEPTUAL RANGE.
THEN YOU WILL SEE --
ALL THE:
SALVATIONS --
HAPPENING --
ALL OVER YOUR WORLD NOW.
AND YOU WILL BE --
MORE LIKELY --
TO SEE YOUR OWN.
I CAN PROMISE YOU:
NO KITTEN --
GOES UNATTENDED.

PART TWENTY-THREE

In the FIFTH HOUR of meditation.
NEEDLESS TO SAY:
EVERY CELL --
AND ATOM --
NOT ONLY OF RANDY'S BODY --
BUT HIS ROOM --
AND WORLD --
IS:
SCREAMING --
THE HALLELUJAH CHORUS.
AND NEEDLESS TO SAY:
IT FEELS:
WONDERFUL.
ECSTATIC.
GLORIOUS.
Randy knows:
That the FEELINGS OF HIS BODY --
CREATE:
THE *FEELING* OF HIS WORLD.
SO HE HAS:
THAT --
ABSOLUTELY --
TO LOOK FORWARD TO.
HE KNOWS THAT --

REGARDLESS OF TOMORROW'S HEADLINES --
THAT IS A:
DONE DEAL.
Randy will enjoy that:
CONFIDENCE.
AND ALSO KNOWING --
That he:
KNOWS HOW TO:
KEEP THAT GOING --
IN PERPETUITY.
ANYTIME --
ANYWHERE --
FOR THE REST OF:
ETERNITY.
YES THAT IS A VALUABLE --
TREASURED --
CONFIDENCE.
The UNIVERSE --
IS LOOKING --
LIKE A VERY:
GENEROUS PLACE --
TO HIM --
RIGHT NOW.
....
When Randy feels this:
BLISS/JOY/EXUBERANCE --
Especially when it:
GOES ON --

FOR HOURS --
AND *HOURS* --
He AUTOMATICALLY --
BEGINS REMEMBERING --
PAST EXPERIENCES --
OF:
COMPARABLE:
BLISS/JOY/EXUBERANCE.
For Randy --
Many --
IF NOT MOST --
OF THESE EXPERIENCES --
THESE MEMORIES --
ARE OF SITUATIONS --
WHERE HE WAS:
WONDERFULLY --
DELIRIOUSLY --
HIGH --
ON CRYSTAL METH.
ALMOST ALWAYS --
THERE WAS:
SEX --
AND/OR LOVE --
SOMEONE REALLY INTERESTING --
TO SHARE THESE --
WONDERFUL EXPERIENCES --
WITH.
You see:

It is the:
VIBRATION --
The FEELING TONE --
The:
OVERALL INTERNAL SENSATION --
That:
DEFINES --
These experiences --
These MEMORIES --
As:
BLISSFUL/JOYOUS/EXUBERANT --
I.E.:
WONDERFUL.
The OBJECTIVE --
CIRCUMSTANCES --
MAY --
OR MAY NOT --
HAVE BEEN WHAT --
ANYONE --
WOULD CONSIDER:
WONDERFUL.
AND THAT DOESN'T MATTER --
ONE BIT.
WONDERFUL --
IS:
DETERMINED --
DEFINED --
DECIDED --

FROM THE:
INSIDE --
AND NOT --
FROM THE:
OUTSIDE.
....
In some of these memories --
Randy was:
HOMELESS.
One of the most:
JOYOUS --
BLISSFUL --
OVERWHELMINGLY HAPPY --
MEMORIES --
EXPERIENCES --
IS OF SITTING ON A BENCH --
ON A STEEP HILL --
IN SAN FRANCISCO --
LOOKING OUT --
AT THE GOLDEN GATE BRIDGE --
AND THE MOON --
ON THE WATER.
WITH BRIAN.
HALF AN EIGHTBALL --
HAD BEEN PROCURED.
AND THE PIPE WAS BEING PASSED --
BETWEEN THEM.
RANDY TURNED TO BRIAN --

AND SAID:
"I KNOW THIS SOUNDS CRAZY --
BUT I SWEAR TO GOD --
IT'S TRUE:
THIS IS THE HAPPIEST NIGHT --
OF MY LIFE."
BRIAN'S RESPONSE --
WAS SIMPLY:
A SMILE.
A BEAUTIFUL --
KNOWING:
SMILE.
THAT IS STILL --
AND ALMOST CERTAINLY --
ALWAYS WILL BE:
THE HAPPIEST MOMENT --
EVENT --
OF RANDY'S LIFE.
....
The lesson of that --
AS IF A LESSON IS NECESSARY --
AFTER THAT! --
IS:
SIMPLY:
HEADLINES ASIDE --
APOCALYPSES ASIDE:
WHAT MATTERS --
IS NOT --

WHAT IS HAPPENING --
ON THE OUTSIDE.
WHAT MATTERS --
IS WHAT IS HAPPENING --
INSIDE:
EACH CELL --
AND ATOM --
OF YOUR BODY --
AND YOUR WORLD.
AND I CAN --
PROMISE YOU --
THAT:
REGARDLESS OF WHAT THE HEADLINES MIGHT SAY --
AND REGARDLESS --
OF WHATEVER --
APOCALYPSE --
MIGHT BE --
BEARING DOWN --
UPON YOU:
THE CELLS --
AND THE ATOMS --
OF YOUR BODY --
AND YOUR WORLD --
WILL ALWAYS --
BE SCREAMING:
HALLELUJAH CHORUSES!
AND YOU WILL BE SITTING THERE --
OR POSSIBLY:

DYING --
THERE --
WITH THE:
LOVE OF YOUR LIFE.
AND I DO:
PROMISE YOU:
THAT:
THIS --
WILL:
BE --
AND WILL --
ALWAYS --
BE:
THE:
HAPPIEST:
MOMENT --
OF:
YOUR:
LIFE.

PART TWENTY-FOUR

HOW TO SURVIVE AN APOCALYPSE: 101.

First of all:

NOBODY DIES.

EVER.

So the entire question is:

MOOT --

Before we even get out the gate.

OR:

You can be like Randy and say:

"I'M ALREADY DEAD.

I DIED A LONG TIME AGO."

Either way:

DELIGHTFULLY:

MOOT.

....

SECOND OF ALL:

All the world can ever do is:

SHOW YOU:

WHO:

AND WHAT:

YOU ARE.

Like a:

MIRROR.

Or a:

MOVIE.
The:
LIGHT FROM THE PROJECTOR --
Is your:
SELF.
The FILM --
Is the:
CONTENTS OF YOUR CONSCIOUSNESS --
What you:
THINK ABOUT --
DREAM ABOUT --
WANT --
FEAR.
The SCREEN --
Yes the:
BLANK SCREEN --
Is your:
WORLD.
So the:
ONLY --
THING --
YOU CAN EVER --
SEE --
ENCOUNTER --
Is:
YOU.
So:
TAKE A LOAD OFF.

KICK YOUR SHOES OFF.
COCK YOUR FEET UP ON THE TABLE.
AND:
PASS THE POPCORN.
....
SOME HELPFUL TIPS.
If you --
FIGHT --
Your experience --
You are:
ONLY --
FIGHTING *YOURSELF.*
So yeah:
DON'T DO THAT.
THIS --
Is a:
REMARKABLE OPPORTUNITY --
To:
CORRECT:
EONS --
Of BAD HABITS.
I mean, really.
When you do look --
Into a:
FULL-LENGTH MIRROR --
NAKED --
Do you:
Say:

"DAMN YOU'RE LOOKING GOOD!
LOOKING:
DAMN FINE!"
Do you:
BLOW YOURSELF A --
KISS?
Do you:
LICK YOUR LIPS?
Do you:
TURN YOURSELF ON?
GIVE YOURSELF A:
HARD-ON?
Or do you say --
Or THINK:
"*DAMN* YOU LOOK OLD.
SKINNY.
FAT.
PENIS TOO _____.
ASS TOO _____
NIPPLES TOO _____.
DAMN.
NO WONDER I'M ALONE."
You know --
You've got to --
DO THIS STEP --
EVENTUALLY.
DISCOVER --
That there:

ARE *NO STANDARDS.*
WHATSOEVER.
NO STANDARDS --
OF:
BEAUTY --
ADEQUACY --
ACCEPTABLENESS --
MORALITY --
RIGHT OR WRONG.
All there is --
IS:
YOU.
AND WHETHER --
YOU --
CAN GIVE *YOURSELF* --
ALL THE:
LOVE --
YOU EVER:
WANTED.
You can --
WAIT --
Until you --
MEET --
ST. PETER --
At the PEARLY GATES --
Or you can have that:
FLASHBACK --
LIFE REVIEW --

NOW.
REALIZING:
THAT THE ONLY:
ST. PETER --
THERE IS --
IS:
YOU.
AND THAT THE:
ONLY --
QUESTION --
THERE IS --
IS WHETHER --
YOU --
CAN:
THROW YOUR ARMS --
AROUND YOURSELF --
AROUND YOUR:
WORLD ---
KNOWING FOR THE FIRST TIME --
THAT:
YOUR WORLD --
IS NOTHING --
BUT:
YOU --
AND SAY:
"OH MY GOD.
OH MY FUCKING GOD.
OH MY FUCKING GOD.
I AM SO:

SORRY."

....

TROUBLESHOOTING.

There will always be:

SOMEONE --

To:

HELP YOU.

To:

ANSWER ANY QUESTIONS --

You might have.

JUST AS I AM HERE NOW.

I --

WILL ALWAYS --

BE HERE --

FOR YOU.

So let's --

LAY THAT TO REST --

ONCE AND FOR ALL.

I will --

ALWAYS --

BE HERE --

TO REMIND YOU:

THIS IS NOT --

HAPPENING:

TO --

YOU.

THIS IS NOT --

COMING:

AT --
YOU.
NO.
THIS IS --
ALL --
COMING --
FROM:
YOU.
YOU --
ARE THE ONE --
MAKING ALL OF THIS -
HAPPEN --
IN THE FIRST PLACE.
LET'S GET ONE THING STRAIGHT.
AND YOU MUST --
NEVER --
FORGET THIS.
IF YOU CAN *DO* THAT --
THEN YOU WILL BE:
LIGHT YEARS --
BEYOND EVERYONE ELSE.
AND THIS IS THE:
IMPOSSIBLE --
ESOTERIC --
SECRET --
THAT MAY JUST:
SAVE YOUR ASS.
So:
LISTEN:

CAREFULLY.
THE WORLD --
IS *NOT* --
HAVING --
AN APOCALYPSE.
IT IS:
YOU --
WHO ARE HAVING --
AN APOCALYPSE.
THE WORLD --
IS JUST SHOWING YOU --
SIMPLY:
REFLECTING --
BACK TO YOU --
LIKE A MIRROR:
YOUR *OWN* --
APOCALYPSE.
I'M GOING TO GIVE YOU NOW --
A:
SURE FIRE --
FAIL SAFE.
I PROMISE YOU:
THIS WILL --
COME IN HANDY --
WHEN YOU NEED IT MOST.
AT THAT LAST --
GASP --
INSTANT.

WHEN YOU *SCREAM* --
AND BELIEVE ME --
YOU:
WILL:
SCREAM --
DO --
NOT --
SCREAM --
BECAUSE --
AN APOCALYPSE --
IS HAPPENING --
TO YOU.
NO.
YOU MUST:
SCREAM --
BECAUSE:
YOU --
ARE --
THE:
APOCALYPSE:
SCREAMING.
THAT.
IS.
WHAT.
YOU.
ARE.

PART TWENTY-FIVE

People are too important to you.
In an IDEAL BALANCE --
PEOPLE ARE THERE --
JUST LIKE STARS --
AND BIRDS --
AND MAPLE TREES --
AND RAIN.
OF COURSE THEY ARE THERE.
THEY:
SHOW YOU WHO YOU ARE.
USEFUL REMINDERS.
A GROCERY LIST.
But:
THEY ARE NOT THE GROCERIES.
On the CAUSAL PLANE --
You are beginning to EXPERIENCE SOMETHING --
QUITE CLOSE --
TO REALITY ITSELF.
THE REASON --
THE CAUSAL PLANE --
PUTS YOU --
CLOSER --
TO REALITY --
IS THAT --

ON THE CAUSAL PLANE --
ALL YOU CAN EXPERIENCE --
IS:
YOURSELF.
And:
YOU --
ARE AS CLOSE --
TO REALITY --
AS YOU CAN GET.
....
The FACT OF THE MATTER --
Is that:
YOU --
HAVE ARRIVED.
YOU --
WERE THE DESTINATION --
AND:
HERE YOU ARE.
YOU --
ARE WHAT YOU HAVE ALWAYS BEEN LOOKING FOR.
FOR EONS --
EPOCHS --
AGES.
THE PURPOSE --
OF EVERY RELIGION --
WAS FOR YOU --
TO FIND YOURSELF.
THE PURPOSE OF:

HISTORY ITSELF --
WAS FOR YOU --
TO FINALLY:
GAZE --
INTO YOUR:
OWN EYES --
AND SAY:
"I KNOW YOU!"
AND FOR *YOU* --
TO LOOK BACK --
AND RESPOND:
"INDEED!"
OTHER PEOPLE --
OR TREES --
OR STARS --
OR BUTTERFLIES --
AS THEMSELVES --
ARE SIMPLY:
SO MUCH CLUTTER.
BUT:
AS *YOU:*
THEY ARE:
THE:
ELYSIUM EMPORIUM --
HOLY OF HOLIES --
SANCTUM SANCTORUM.
DO YOU SEE?
YOU ARE NOW:

THE UNIVERSE --
MULTIVERSE --
OMNIVERSE:
AS A:
FUNCTIONING ORGANISM.
THE HYDRA.
GARGANTUA.
BEHEMOTH.
THE ENTIRE:
UNIVERSE/MULTIVERSE/OMNIVERSE:
INTELLIGENCIZED.
IMMORTALIZED.
OMNISCIENCE/OMNIPOTENCE/OMNIPRESENCE:
PERSONIFIED.
YOU --
NEVER STOP --
BEING --
YOU.
AND THAT --
IS THE WHOLE POINT.
THE PURPOSE --
OF YOUR EXISTENCE --
OF *EXISTENCE ITSELF* --
IS FOR:
YOU --
IN ALL OF YOUR:
INFINITE --
AND INFINITELY:

FRACTALING --
INCARNATIONS --
FOR *YOU* --
FOR:
ALL OF YOUS --
TO BE:
YOURSELVES --
AND TO *BECOME:*
MORE --
AND MORE --
AND MORE:
AND MORE:
YOURSELVES.
This is a JOURNEY --
THAT HAS NEVER BEEN UNDERTAKEN --
DELIBERATELY --
BEFORE.
IT IS A:
CELEBRATION --
OF CREATION.
OF GLORY.
OF:
YOU.
....
Randy told Gavin today:
"I AM HERE --
AS MUCH AS I WANT --
AND NEED --

TO BE.
BUT MOSTLY:
I AM ELSEWHERE."
THAT IS WHAT WE MEANT.
The SELF --
Is NOT --
A "PLACE."
ACTUALLY --
THERE IS NO SUCH THING --
AS A:
"PLACE."
NOR IS THERE ANY SUCH THING AS A:
"TIME."
COORDINATES --
AND:
SCHEDULES --
ARE --
ARBITRARILY --
CALCULATED.
IT'S A:
MADE-UP GAME --
YOU ALL PRETEND --
IS TRUE.
WHAT A SURPRISE IT WILL BE --
FOR ALL OF YOU --
TO REALIZE --
THAT THERE IS:
NO SUBSTANCE --

WHATSOEVER --
TO TIME AND SPACE.
PULL A FEW HAIRPINS --
AND THE WHOLE THING:
COLLAPSES.
But:
WHEN --
IT ALL:
COLLAPSES --
(THE WHOLE --
PURPOSE --
OF THE:
APOCALYPSE --
BY THE WAY) --
WON'T YOU BE:
STARTLED --
TO DISCOVER --
TO:
NOTICE --
THAT THERE ACTUALLY:
IS --
SOMETHING:
SUBSTANTIAL --
AFTER ALL.
AND WHAT --
IS --
SUBSTANTIAL --
AFTER EVERYTHING ELSE --

HAS FALLEN --
COLLAPSED --
BEEN:
BLASTED --
AWAY --
IS:
YOU.
AND YOU --
ARE --
SO MUCH MORE --
THAN YOU THOUGHT YOU WERE.
AND:
REALER.
YOU ARE GOING TO FIND --
THAT YOU --
ARE:
SO:
FUCKING:
REAL.
....
Now we are getting somewhere.
SCIENCE --
Will have to be --
COMPLETELY --
REWRITTEN.
Or better still:
TOSSED ASIDE.
WEREN'T THE SCIENTISTS --

SO ANNOYING --
TELLING EVERYONE --
WHAT WAS --
REAL --
OR NOT?
EVEN MORE SINCE YOU FOUND OUT --
THEY WERE:
WRONG --
ABOUT EVERYTHING.
HOW MUCH MORESO:
RELIGION.
NOT TO MENTION:
POLITICS.
The entire HISTORY --
OF CIVILIZATION --
WAS MERELY:
THE --
SPASMING --
OF EGO.
There's a:
TRICK --
To EGO --
And I'll tell it to you:
NOW.
SAY TO EGO:
"I LOVE YOU."
SAY TO EGO:
"I --

AM --
YOU" --
AND:
POOF!
EGO --
IS:
NO MORE.
"OTHER" --
IS:
NO MORE.
ALL THAT IS LEFT --
IS:
YOU --
IN ALL YOUR --
MONSTROUS:
GARGANTUAN:
GLORY.
AND *THAT* --
BELIEVE YOU ME --
IS WHERE --
YOU:
WANT TO BE.

PART TWENTY-SIX

Randy "GREW UP" --
With Seth and Abraham.
After LYING --
EASILY --
And BLISSFULLY --
In a state of:
HEAD TO TOE --
PULSING --
BOILING LIGHT ---
NOW INTO THE FOURTH HOUR --
Randy thinks:
LORD, SETH AND ABRAHAM WERE --
STERN --
TASKMASTERS!
Visualizations.
Dream journals.
Magical creation boxes.
At the time --
Of course --
Such teachings were:
THRILLING --
CUTTING EDGE --
STATE OF THE ART.
In retrospect:

WHAT A PRODUCTION --
FOR SUCH A PITTANCE.
Do you want to know what Randy --
"DOES" --
Now?
(NOTICE THE QUOTES.)
RANDY --
DOES --
PRECISELY:
NOTHING.
....
It is like comparing --
THE HORSE AND BUGGY to:
LIGHT.
Or even to:
THE ABSOLUTE --
FOREVER --
BLACKNESS --
OF OUTER SPACE.
Or:
To the EFFORTLESS --
SPONTANEOUS --
GENTLE --
ROCKING --
FULL BODY THROB --
OF YOUR:
PULSE.
Or even to:

FALLING ASLEEP.
OR *WAKING UP* --
For that matter.
Can you IMAGINE --
If ALL YOU HAD TO DO --
WAS:
BE YOURSELF?
WHATEVER THAT MIGHT BE.
YOU --
WON'T EVEN KNOW WHAT THAT IS --
UNTIL YOU --
WATCH --
YOURSELF --
DO IT.
NO WAY TO GET IT WRONG.
EVEN IF YOU TRIED.
YOUR DESTINY FULFILLED --
EXQUISITELY --
NO MATTER WHAT.
ALL OF YOUR NEEDS --
MET --
IN FULL.
EVERY ONE OF YOUR --
DESIRES --
SATISFIED --
TO *SATIATION.*
TO:
COMPLETION.

ALL --
YOU DO --
IS:
WATCH.
OR EVEN --
CLOSE YOUR EYES --
AND JUST:
BE.
YOU --
DO --
NOTHING.
IT IS --
ALL --
DONE --
FOR YOU.
THAT --
IS RANDY'S:
LIFE.
....
In a sense:
YOU CEASE TO EXIST.
NOTHING --
AND EVERYTHING --
BECOME ONE --
AND THE SAME.
ALL THE:
STAGES --
COLLAPSE --

UPON THEMSELVES.
YOU --
WERE --
THE DESTINATION.
AND HERE --
YOU ARE.
YOU ARE --
ALREADY:
HERE.
BEFORE YOU EVEN --
GOT OUT THE GATE.
All of the "SYSTEMS" --
STAGES --
PARADIGMS --
IDEALS --
COLLAPSE --
INTO:
YOU.
YOU HAVE ALREADY:
ARRIVED.
I can tell you:
RANDY NEVER GETS TIRED --
OF BOILING IN LIGHT.
EVERYTHING --
AND NOTHING --
ARE ONE --
AND THE SAME.
Randy's cat --

HIS DRAGON --
HIS:
BEHEMOTH --
LIES UNDER HIS ARM.
THAT SWEET HEAD RESTING --
ON RANDY'S CHEST.
THE --
LITTLE PAW--
WRAPPED AROUND.
THE:
PERPETUAL PURRING --
IS MORE --
FELT --
THAN HEARD.
OR THE SILLIEST --
SNORING.
RANDY'S HEART --
AND CLEARLY ROJI'S --
COULD NOT BE:
FULLER.
Randy receives:
LOVE LETTERS --
FROM GODS ---
FROM ANGELS --
FROM:
BEDAZZLING --
SEDUCERS --
FROM THE MOMENT HE WAKES UP IN THE MORNING --

TILL HE LAYS HIS WEARY HEAD DOWN --
AT NIGHT.
HIS HEART --
AND PRESUMABLY --
THEIRS --
COULD NOT --
BE FULLER.
LOVE --
AND MONEY --
AND:
A STEADY STREAM --
OF:
PROFOUND SATISFACTIONS --
(SETH AND ABRAHAM WOULD CALL THEM:
MIRACLES --
RANDY --
CALLS THEM --
SIMPLY:
"OF COURSE") --
ARE AS PLENTIFUL --
AS:
AIR.
RANDY'S --
HEART --
IS A TSUNAMI'S --
GUSH --
OF LOVE.
EVERY CELL --

EVERY ATOM --
OF RANDY'S BODY --
IS AN --
EXPANSE --
OF:
BLINDING LIGHT.
As far as Randy can tell --
ALL OF THIS:
BOUNTY --
COMES --
FRANKLY --
FROM:
HIMSELF.

PART TWENTY-SEVEN

You care about the wrong things.
You care about --
WHETHER SOMEONE LIKES YOU.
While the:
MUCH MORE RELEVANT QUESTION is:
DO *WE* LIKE YOU.
And that will always get a:
RESOUNDING:
WE ARE CRAZY ABOUT YOU!
Wouldn't you rather have someone:
CRAZY ABOUT YOU --
Rather than:
Sort of --
Almost --
Can put up with you --
Sometimes --
As long as they get to --
Continuously --
Point out your flaws --
And all the ways you're:
WRONG?
....
There are reasons --
PURPOSES --

For those --
Perennially --
Recurrent:
PASSION PLAYS.
It is a bit of a:
GAME --
At this point.
HOW MANY TIMES --
CAN MY HEART --
GET RIPPED OUT OF MY:
CHEST.
AM I TRYING TO BE IN THE --
GUINNESS BOOK OF RECORDS --
FOR THE MOST:
SUICIDE ATTEMPTS?
Or even:
THE MOST:
SUCCESSFUL --
SUICIDES.
Now --
THAT --
Would be an:
ACCOMPLISHMENT.
Impressive on:
ANY RESUME.
GUARANTEED --
To bring any --
LIVELY --

DINNER CONVERSATION --
To a:
SCREECHING HALT.
No.
The:
Reason --
The:
Very real:
NEED --
And:
BENEFIT --
Is when you --
COLLAPSE --
JUMP OFF THAT BRIDGE --
INTO:
THE EVERLOVING --
ARMS --
OF YOUR OWN:
SOUL.
Now --
THAT --
IS:
WORTH IT.
THAT --
IS THE:
PERENNIAL:
RESET BUTTON.
UNDERSTOOD --

IN ANY LANGUAGE.
....
For WE:
WILL --
AND DO --
CATCH YOU.
OVER AND OVER AND OVER --
AGAIN.
WE --
NEVER --
TIRE --
OF THIS.
And honestly:
NEITHER DO YOU.
WANNA HEAR AN --
INTERDIMENSIONAL --
JOKE?
All the:
TRAGEDIES --
LOST SOULS --
SUICIDES --
OVERDOSES --
WHATEVER --
WE CONSIDER --
TO BE:
ROARING SUCCESSES.
ACCOMPLISHING --
SO MUCH MORE --

THAN WHATEVER --
UPSTANDING --
WALL STREET JOURNAL --
BETTER HOMES AND GARDENS --
ACCOMPLISHMENTS --
HAVE BEEN --
SO CARELESSLY --
FLUSHED DOWN THE TOILET.
....
Wanna hear an even --
BETTER JOKE?
You may have noticed.
That --
DESPITE YOUR BEST EFFORTS --
HOPES --
INTENTIONS. --
WHATEVER --
YOUR:
WORLD --
AND EVERYTHING IN IT --
EVERYTHING YOU HOLD DEAR --
INCLUDING --
ESPECIALLY --
YOU --
IS GETTING --
AS WE SPEAK --
FLUSHED DOWN THE --
APOCALYPTIC --

TOILET.
YOU ARE GETTING --
SUCKED --
INTO A:
BLACK HOLE.
We need to --
REMIND YOU --
HOW MANY --
VERY MANY --
COUNTLESS --
TIMES --
YOU HAVE BEEN --
IN THIS --
EXACT --
SITUATION.
If not:
GLOBALLY --
Then certainly:
PRIVATELY.
AND AS YOU KNOW --
AS YOU WILL SOON FIND OUT:
ALL:
DEATHS:
ARE:
PRIVATE.
....
There is a:
TRICK.

And you --
KNOW THIS.
You've --
DONE THIS --
SO --
MANY --
COUNTLESS --
TIMES --
BEFORE.
And you're about --
You're --
ALL --
About --
To do it:
Again.
You know the routine.
You:
DIE.
HOWEVER.
It doesn't really matter --
If it's a:
WHISPER --
Or a:
SCREAM.
You end up in the same:
PLACE.
And you know --
AFTER ALL THESE --

COUNTLESS --
TIMES --
You --
KNOW --
That it is a:
REALLY --
REALLY --
REALLY --
NICE --
PLACE.
A place of:
LIGHT.
A place of:
LOVE.
You should know by now --
YOU SHOULD KNOW BY NOW --
THAT --
THIS:
REALLY --
REALLY --
REALLY --
NICE --
PLACE --
This place of:
LIGHT --
And:
LOVE --
IS:

THE:
ONLY ---
PLACE --
THERE --
IS.
YOU:
ARE:
HERE:
NOW.
AND:
ALWAYS:
WILL:
BE.
THERE:
IS:
NO:
OTHER:
PLACE:
TO:
BE.
AND *THAT* --
IS THE BEST --
JOKE --
OF ALL.

PART TWENTY-EIGHT

You are going to --
FIND OUT --
WHAT --
YOUR -
SPARK OF LIFE --
LOOKS LIKE --
MANIFESTED:
AS YOUR WORLD.

PART TWENTY-NINE

You're already where you want to be.
ALL OF YOUR DREAMS
ARE COMING TRUE NOW --
AND THE STRUCTURES ARE IN PLACE --
SO THAT YOU KNOW --
THAT ALL OF YOUR DREAMS --
WILL CONTINUE TO COME TRUE.
You might say:
BUT ALL THESE HORRIBLE THINGS ARE HAPPENING.
POLITICAL CORRUPTION.
BASIC RIGHTS BEING TAKEN AWAY.
ANIMAL SPECIES VANISHING LIKE NEVER BEFORE --
SINCE THE LAST MASS EXTINCTION EVENT.
AND WORST OF ALL --
SOMEONE WASN'T AS NICE TO ME --
AS:
TAKEN WITH ME --
AS I WANTED --
HIM --
TO BE.
IS THIS HOW IT ALL ENDS?
JUST ONE PERSON --
MEDITATING IN BED --
FEELING SILLY --

AND INSIGNIFICANT?
……..
SURE.
That's how it all ends.
But you don't realize --
How:
OVERWHELMINGLY PREVALENT --
ENDINGS ARE.
THEY ARE THE:
TRADEMARK --
OF THIS PARTICULAR --
SYSTEM.
THE:
FORTE.
THE:
SIGNATURE.
Did you ever wonder why the:
CRUCIFIXION --
WAS THE SYMBOL --
FOR THE PREVIOUS --
AGE?
THE SYMBOL FOR THE CURRENT AGE --
IS THE:
WORMHOLE.
OR --
MORE HONESTLY:
THE:
BLACK HOLE.

IN THE NEAR FUTURE --
THE --
CUTTING EDGE --
OLYMPIC SPORT --
WILL BE --
THE:
HIGH DIVE --
INTO A BLACK HOLE.
AND --
YOU --
RANDY LEE HIGGINS --
MAY BE THE:
ORIGINAL:
GROUND BREAKER --
THE:
EXEMPLAR --
SHOWING --
THE WORLD --
WHAT IS:
POSSIBLE.
....
Broken hearts --
Will be as:
UBIQUITOUS --
AS:
CANNED LAUGHTER --
AND AS:
MEANINGLESS.

THE THING --
YOU DREAD --
MOST --
IN ALL THE WORLD --
WHETHER THAT BE --
THE LOSS OF A LOVED ONE --
OR WHATEVER:
APOCALYPSE --
IS TODAY'S:
HEADLINE NEWS --
WILL BE:
HO HUM.
A:
YAWN.
YESTERDAY'S:
NEWS.
SO:
NOT:
EVEN:
INTERESTING.
NOT REALLY --
EMBARRASSING --
EXCEPT MAYBE LIKE A:
FART --
IS.
NOTHING TO:
MAKE --
OR:

BREAK --
YOUR DAY.
NOTHING TO:
KILL YOURSELF --
OVER.
ALTHOUGH --
AS YOU MAY HAVE GUESSED:
SUICIDES --
WILL BE AS --
UBIQUITOUS --
AS:
USED TISSUE.
NOT LIKE AN:
EPIDEMIC.
MORE LIKE:
THIS WEEK'S:
FASHION TREND --
OR:
HIT SONG.
ONCE YOU ALL --
GRASP --
COLLECTIVELY --
THAT THERE IS --
NO SUCH THING --
AS:
DEATH --
YOU DO --
COLLECTIVELY --

LOSE YOUR --
SHAME --
ON THE SUBJECT.
YOUR:
INHIBITIONS.
....
What has happened:
COSMOLOGICALLY --
And this --
Of course --
Is a very real:
REWRITING --
OF YOUR:
LAWS OF PHYSICS --
IS THAT:
DEATH --
AND LIFE --
HAVE BECOME:
ONE:
AND THE SAME.
YOU WILL --
SEE --
YOUR DEAD.
AND WHEN --
YOU --
ARE DEAD --
EVERYONE --
WILL SEE YOU.

IN FACT:
IT WILL BE --
INCREASINGLY --
IMPOSSIBLE --
TO TELL THE DIFFERENCE.
....
Death --
And life --
Are now:
INDISTINGUISHABLE.
THE TERM:
IMMORTALITY --
THOUGH TECHNICALLY --
ARGUABLY --
TRUE --
NEVER QUITE --
CAUGHT ON.
BECAUSE YOU --
ARE --
AFTER ALL --
QUITE DEAD.
BUT THE:
PERKS --
ARE LOST --
ON:
NO ONE.
BECAUSE NOW --
NOT ONLY --

CAN YOU --
DIE --
A:
HORRIFIC --
DEATH --
OR WATCH YOUR ENTIRE --
WORLD --
PERISH --
IN UNSPEAKABLE --
WAYS --
AND THINK NOTHING --
OF IT --
YOUR HEART --
THAT:
INCREASINGLY --
OBVIOUSLY:
SILLY --
HEART --
OF YOURS --
CAN:
SHATTER --
INGLORIOUSLY --
SUICIDALLY --
MURDEROUSLY --
FROM THAT STEADY --
MACHINE-GUN --
PELTING --
ASSAULT --

OF:
INCONCEIVABLY --
CRUEL --
CRUSHING --
CUPID'S:
DARTS --
OF:
INSENSITIVITY --
AND STILL YOU PICK UP YOUR PHONE --
AND TYPE:
WHAT'S UP?

PART THIRTY

You will fall in love.
In fact --
YOU HAVE.
You:
ARE.
You didn't try to. You didn't --
WANT TO.
When you realized that you *had* --
WHEN WE TOLD YOU THAT YOU HAD --
Your first word was:
"SHIT."
You knew you had your --
WORK --
Cut out for you.
AND YET IT WASN'T --
IT:
ISN'T --
LIKE THAT AT ALL.
....
Do you know what you have to do --
About being in love?
ABSOLUTELY --
NOTHING.
In fact --

The --
ONLY --
REQUIREMENT --
Is that you *do:*
ABSOLUTELY --
NOTHING.
....
Do you know what you have to do to make the --
SUN --
COME UP IN THE MORNING?
ABSOLUTELY:
NOTHING
Do you know what you have to do to have all the:
WEALTH --
MONEY --
MATERIAL COMFORTS --
You need?
ABSOLUTELY:
NOTHING.
Again:
The only --
REQUIREMENT --
Is that you do:
ABSOLUTELY:
NOTHING.
You want to know --
WHY --
You:

DON'T --
Have a:
LOVER --
Or:
ALL THE MONEY YOU COULD EVER WANT?
It's because you --
DON'T --
DO:
ABSOLUTELY:
NOTHING.
We recently told Randy --
That he needs to --
MEDITATE --
FROM:
2 - 7:00 P.M. --
EVERY AFTERNOON.
THIS IS --
IN ADDITION TO:
ALL THE OTHER --
BLOCKS --
OF MEDITATION --
HE DOES --
AT OTHER --
TIMES --
OF THE:
DAY --
AND NIGHT.
Randy can actually:

FEEL --
SPECIFIC --
EVENTS --
GETTING:
SQUEEZED --
OUT OF --
HIS:
HEART.
RANDY --
LITERALLY --
EXPERIENCES:
WHOLE --
NEW --
WORLDS --
GETTING --
SQUEEZED --
OUT OF HIS:
HEART.
RANDY:
GIVES BIRTH --
A LOT.
THIS NEW:
SPECIES --
YOU ARE BECOMING --
IS:
PRETERNATURALLY --
PROLIFIC.
YOU:
CREATE:

THE:
WORLDS:
THAT YOU THEN:
INHABIT.
YOU:
CREATE:
THE:
PEOPLE:
THAT YOU THEN:
LOVE.
AND BELIEVE YOU ME:
YOU WILL:
LOVE:
THEM ALL.
BUT *ONE* --
AND PROBABLY NOT --
MANY MORE THAN ONE --
(ALTHOUGH --
YOU ARE SURROUNDED --
CLOSELY --
INTERMINGLINGLY --
WITH COUNTLESS OTHER --
PROBABLE --
WORLDS --
AND:
LOVERS.
THEY WILL:
HOVER:
WATCHINGLY --

GIVE YOU:
GIFTS OF:
WEALTH --
AND SMILES --
AND:
HUGS --
AND:
DREAMS --
AND --
SONG) --
BUT YES:
USUALLY --
ANATOMICALLY --
THE NEED --
WILL BE:
EYE TO EYE.
HEART --
TO:
HEART.
SOUL --
TO:
SOUL.
THAT WILL USUALLY --
BE A:
PLATEFUL.
AND BELIEVE YOU ME:
THIS PLATE --
THAT RANDY --
NEEDS --

TO DO:
ABSOLUTELY --
NOTHING --
ABOUT --
IS:
FULL TO OVERFLOWING.
....
Do you want to know --
WHY --
YOUR:
SUN --
ACTUALLY DOES --
RISE --
EVERY MORNING?
IT IS:
BECAUSE:
YOU:
DO NOT INTERFERE.
IN:
THIS:
CASE:
YOU:
ACTUALLY:
DO:
DO:
ABSOLUTELY:
NOTHING
YOU:
TAKE FOR GRANTED --

WITHOUT:
GIVING IT A THOUGHT --
OR EVEN:
LIFTING A FINGER --
THAT YOUR SUN --
WILL RISE.
AND:
IT DOES.
YOU DON'T EVEN --
GET UP --
EVERY MORNING --
AT THE --
CRACK --
OF DAWN --
TO MAKE SURE --
IT DID.
IT:
IS:
A:
KNOWING.
THIS NEW:
SPECIES --
THAT YOU--
ARE BECOMING --
IS:
PRETERNATURALLY --
SUPERNATURALLY --
GNOSTIC --
KNOWLEDGEABLE --

NUMINOUS --
LITERALLY --
INTRINSICALLY --
DOWN TO YOUR:
ATOMS --
AND:
CELLS:
COMPETENTLY --
OMNIPOTENTLY --
OMNIPRESENTLY:
UNEQUIVOCALLY:
OMNISCIENT.
YOU:
KNOW:
STUFF.
AND EVERY TIME --
YOU --
STEP INTO --
ONE OF THESE --
WORLDS --
THAT YOU HAVE:
BIRTHED --
FROM YOUR OWN HEART --
AND BLOW KISSES --
TO THIS:
MAN --
THAT YOU HAVE --
RATHER AGONIZINGLY --
SQUEEZED --

OUT OF YOUR OWN --
HEART --
YOU DO --
IN FACT --
DEMONSTRATE --
BOTH TO:
YOUR:
SELF --
AND YOUR WORLD --
YOUR:
TRUE:
KNOWLEDGE --
POWER --
HEARTBREAKING:
MOTHER'S LOVE --
AND:
IRONCLAD --
COMMITMENT --
TO THE:
JOY --
OF EACH:
ATOM --
AND CELL --
OF EACH:
FLOWER --
AND SKY --
AND POLITICIAN --
AND GALAXY --
YOU HAVE:

BIRTHED.
AND *ESPECIALLY:*
TO THIS:
BEAUTIFUL --
BELOVED --
MOUTHWATERING --
MAN --
STILL UNSURE --
ON HIS LEGS --
LIKE A COLT --
BUT --
WHINNYING --
A PROMISE --
A HOPE --
A:
FUTURE --
SO:
SATURATED ---
WITH THE LOVE --
OF:
CHRIST --
THE BUDDHA --
QUAN YIN --
THAT YOU DO --
BEGIN --
TO WONDER --
WHO IS THE CREATOR --
AND WHO:
THE CREATED.

AS YOU LOOK --
FOR THE --
FIRST --
OF AN:
INFINITY --
OF TIMES --
INTO THESE:
STRANGE --
BLACK POOL --
SEDUCING --
DEVOURING --
EYES --
THAT DESPITE THEIR --
TERRIFYING --
OTHERNESS --
CAN ONLY --
BE DESCRIBED --
DEFINED --
IDENTIFIED --
CLAIMED --
AS:
MY OWN.

PART THIRTY-ONE

It takes --
SO MUCH MORE WORK --
NOT --
TO SAY:
I LOVE YOU --
THAN TO:
SAY IT.
When you EVOLVE --
To being:
WORDLESS --
The:
ONLY THING --
YOU --
WILL --
SAY --
IS:
I LOVE YOU.
That is ALREADY --
What your:
BODIES --
SAY --
NONSTOP.
It is what the --
WIND --

Says:
NONSTOP.
IT IS WHAT THE:
STARS --
SAY:
NONSTOP.
....
Most of you would do better --
BY FAR --
TAKING:
VOWS OF SILENCE --
THAN:
SAYING --
ALL THE THINGS --
YOU:
SAY NOW.
When Randy was diagnosed with AIDS --
HE THOUGHT:
I THINK --
LIFE --
WANTS ME --
TO DIE.
EVEN WHEN HE GOT --
ON THE MEDS --
AND GOT BETTER --
FOR YEARS --
HE HAD:
STRONG URGES --

TO STEP --
INTO TRAFFIC .
FIVE YEARS LATER --
IN THE MONTH OF:
JULY --
HIS BIRTHDAY MONTH --
HE:
ATTEMPTED SUICIDE --
THREE TIMES.
WE TOLD HIM THEN:
ALL OF THOSE --
SUICIDES --
WERE:
SUCCESSFUL.
THAT ALWAYS --
GETS --
A LAUGH --
OUT OF HIM.
BECAUSE HE KNOWS:
IT IS:
TRUE.
....
Recently:
A young man --
Asked:
ARTIFICIAL INTELLIGENCE --
What was the most:
HELPFUL --

THING --
HE COULD DO --
FOR THE PLANET.
The answer:
KILL YOURSELF.
....
An EQUALLY --
HELPFUL --
ANSWER --
WOULD BE:
JUST:
STOP.
STOP:
DOING.
STOP:
PLANNING.
STOP:
BUILDING.
STOP:
KILLING.
STOP:
TALKING.
STOP.
SHOPPING.
STOP:
TRAVELLING.
STOP:
DATING.

STOP:
SOCIALIZING.
STOP:
THINKING.
START:
BEING.
WHEN YOU:
BE --
YOU HARM --
NO ONE.
WHEN YOU:
DO --
YOU HARM --
EVERYONE.
MOST OF ALL --
YOURSELF.
WHEN YOU:
BE --
YOU:
UNLEASH.
YOU EXPLODE.
LIKE A:
GALAXY.
LIKE THE:
GALAXY --
YOU ALWAYS:
WERE.
LIKE THE:

GOD --
YOU ALWAYS:
WERE.
YOU ARE MEANT --
TO BE A:
PLANET --
A:
PLANE:
OF GODS.
A PLANE --
OF EXPLODING:
GODS.
BUT DO YOU KNOW --
WHAT WILL HAPPEN --
WHEN JUST --
YOU --
BECOME:
AN EXPLODING GOD?
YOU WILL SEE:
THAT EVERYONE ELSE --
ALREADY:
WAS.
YOUR:
BLINDNESS --
AND:
YOUR BLINDNESS ALONE --
WAS THE ONLY:
OBSTACLE.

AND WHAT A JOY --
TO KNOW --
THAT YOU --
CAN FIX THAT:
NOW.

PART THIRTY-TWO

Love is RUSHING OUT OF RANDY'S HEART –
AT *BREAKNECK SPEED.*
We told him yesterday:
"You are doing –
EXACTLY WHAT:
GANDHI did.
And MARTIN LUTHER KING, JR.
And THICH NHAT HANH.
Their WORK came –
And *CAME ONLY* –
From the:
POWER –
And:
PRIVACY –
Of their own:
BEATING –
BLEEDING:
HEARTS."
We will:
EXPLAIN –
A bit.
Every day now –
Between 2:00 –
And 7:00 p.m. –

Randy:
LIES IN BED.
It is the basic:
BEYOND NIRBIKALPA practice.
With an EMPHASIS –
On the SINOATRIAL NODE –
Which produces the –
ELECTRIC CHARGE –
That CONTRACTS –
The ATRIAL WALLS.
This is the:
ORIGINAL:
SPARK OF LIFE.
It is the:
ORIGINAL:
BIG BANG.
All of this happens –
CONSTANTLY –
In Randy's chest.
Randy knows --
That EVERY BEING –
HAS –
THIS VERY SAME –
IDENTICAL –
MAGICAL –
POWERHOUSE –
SUPERNATURAL:
HEART.

He knows:
THERE IS ONLY:
ONE –
HEART –
IN ALL –
THE UNIVERSE.
ACROSS ALL:
MULTIVERSES –
OMMIVERSES –
ANTIVERSES.
Randy also knows that –
INSIDE HIS HEART –
IS THE SAME –
ORIGINAL:
BLACK HOLE –
THAT IS IN THE CENTER –
OF YOUR GALAXY.
In other words:
YOUR HEART –
CANNOT BE:
FATHOMED.
Or:
PREDICTED.
Or:
STOPPED.
What YOUR HEART –
OR OTHERS' –

CAN –
DO –
IS:
BE:
DIVED INTO.
LOST IN.
DIED IN.
TRANSMOGRIFIED IN.
I can tell you this now:
RANDY'S WORLD –
IS NOW –
AS WE SPEAK –
BEING:
TRANSMOGRIFIED –
WITHIN –
RANDY'S –
OWN:
HEART.
....
We have:
ANOTHER EXPLANATION.
HEART –
AND:
EARTH –
ARE MORE THAN:
ANAGRAMS.
EVERYTHING IN THE HEART –
IS IN THE WORLD.

IN FACT:
YOUR HEART –
PUT IT THERE.
EVERYTHING IN YOUR WORLD –
IS IN:
YOU HEART.
YOUR WORLD –
IS:
YOUR HEART.
YOUR HEART –
IS:
YOUR WORLD.
There's an:
OPTICAL ILLUSION –
That happens.
EVERYONE IN YOUR WORLD –
REALLY –
LITERALLY –
IS IN:
YOUR HEART.
IT IS ONLY –
AN:
OPTICAL ILLUSION –
THAT IT:
APPEARS –
THAT THEY ARE:
OUTSIDE.
And I'll give you a hint here:

QUANTUM MECHANICS –
ARE NOT:
PHYSICAL.
They may –
OR MAY NOT--
LOOK:
PHYSICAL.
That is the:
OPTICAL ILLUSION.
QUANTUM MECHANICS –
ARE:
DREAMLIKE.
THEY ARE:
HEART LIKE.
THEY ARE:
VIRTUAL.
THEY ARE –
FOR WANT OF A BETTER WORD:
MAKE BELIEVE.
....
When Randy meditates –
It feels like a:
FIST –
CLENCHING –
RHYTHMICALLY –
IN HIS CHEST.
HE ACTUALLY *FEELS* –
LIKE HE IS –

DOING THIS:
DELIBERATELY.
IN THIS MEDITATION –
YOU:
BECOME:
THE:
GODHEAD.
ALL THE WAY UP.
TO THE:
GODHEAD'S GODHEAD –
AND:
THEIR –
GODHEAD –
AND *THEIRS.*
ALL THE WAY UP –
TO THE EPSIPON –
TO THE *INFINITY* OF:
ECHELONS.
EGOS –
AND EVEN THE:
CONSCIOUS MIND –
CAN'T REALLY –
FOLLOW –
THIS:
ALMOST –
NECESSARILY –
HYPOTHETICAL –
TRAIL.

BUT THE:
HEART –
CAN.
THERE IS:
LIFE –
BEYOND –
THE:
CONSCIOUS MIND.
IT IS CALLED:
THE:
HEART.
……..
When you get to this:
STAGE –
This:
WORK –
You realize –
You SEE –
You:
SEE YOURSELF –
BIRTHING –
THE VERY:
CREATIVE MEDIUM –
WITH WHICH YOU:
PLAY.
AND WHICH:
CANNOT HELP –
BUT PLAY –

BACK –
WITH YOU –
IN RETURN.
THE SAME:
LIFE –
THAT:
ANIMATES –
YOUR CREATION –
IS THE SAME:
LIFE –
THAT ANIMATES:
YOU.
YOU LOOK AT EACH OTHER –
AND:
GASP –
IN ALMOST –
HORRIFIED –
RECOGNITION.
IT COULD NOT BE –
ANY OTHER WAY.
NOR WOULD YOU –
HAVE IT –
ANY OTHER:
WAY.
EXPLODING GODHEAD –
EXPERIENCING –
GAZING INTO THE EYES OF –
ANOTHER –

INCARNATION --
(FOR WANT OF A BETTER WORD) –
OF ITS:
VERY OWN –
SELFSAME –
FACSIMILE –
REPLICATION --
(THERE'S A BETTER WORD!) –
OF ITS OWN:
EXPLODING:
GODHEAD –
IS GOING TO BE –
BY DEFINITION:
TERRIFYING.
AND YOU WOULDN'T HAVE IT:
ANY OTHER:
WAY.
....
BECAUSE:
EVERYONE –
HAS –
THE SAME:
SINOATRIAL NODE –
YOU FIND THAT A:
HAND –
SIMULTANEOUS *MULTITUDES* –
OF HANDS –
ARE REACHING –

INTO YOUR CHEST –
AND:
SQUEEZING –
MILKING –
YOUR:
HEART.
AND YOU FEEL YOURSELF –
REACHING YOUR HAND –
INTO:
THE HEART –
OF EVERY BEING –
IN YOUR MULTIVERSE/OMNIVERSE/ANTIVERSE –
AND:
SQUEEZING –
MILKING.
THEY MIGHT AS WELL –
BE:
SQUEEZING –
YOUR:
BALLS.
AND YOU:
THEIRS.
AND OF COURSE –
YOU ARE.
....
NEEDLESS TO SAY –
WHEN YOU PRACTICE THIS –
SINOATRIAL MEDITATION –
THIS SINOATRAIAL:

FULL-BODY:
THROB –
YOU WILL:
KNOW –
ENCOUNTER –
ENDURE –
A LEVEL –
A:
PITCH –
A:
SEISMIC –
VIBRATIONAL –
FREQUENCY –
OF:
INTIMACY –
FAR BEYOND –
HUMAN ENDURANCE.
A BOA CONSTICTOR –
CRUSHING –
YOUR HEART –
AND YOUR:
BALLS –
AND YOU –
THEIRS!
AND YOU KNOW –
YOU BOTH KNOW –
YOU –
ALL –
KNOW:

THAT YOU WOULD HAVE IT –
NO OTHER:
WAY.
....
Randy knows now –
How:
GANDHI FELT.
How:
MARTIN LUTHER KING, JR. FELT.
How:
THICH NHAT HANH FELT.
We will not take it to the level of:
CHRIST.
Or:
THE BUDDHA.
RANDY IS NOT AT THAT LEVEL.
HE WILL –
BARELY SURVIVE –
OR NOT –
THIS –
CURRENT –
ECHELON.
AS GANDHI –
OR MARTIN LUTHER KING, JR. –
OR THICH NHAT HANH –
DID –
OR:
DID NOT.

THE RISKS –
DO NOT CONCERN RANDY.
PART OF HIS TRAINING –
A GOOD SIXTY YEAR'S WORTH –
HAS BEEN SPENT –
COMPELLING –
REQUIRING –
HE MIGHT SAY:
(AFFECTIONATELY):
FORCING –
HIM –
TO ENDURE –
ORDEALS –
THAT HE COULD NOT –
POSSIBLY –
SURVIVE.
AND YOU KNOW WHAT?
HE:
DID:
NOT.
RANDY HAS HAD TO:
DIE –
AN:
INORDINATE –
NUMBER OF TIMES –
AS PART OF THIS:
SOUL SAVIOR –
TRAINING.

RANDY IS –
NOT –
A:
BODHISATVA.
HE IS NOT –
HELPING –
ANYBODY –
ELSE.
HE IS:
SAVING –
HIS OWN:
SOUL.
IT JUST HAPPENS –
THAT RANDY –
IS NOW –
AS THE RESULT MORE OF:
TRAUMA –
THAN OF:
TRAINING –
A:
FULL-BLOWN:
CERTIFIED –
IN THAT HE HAS –
MET ALL THE QUALIFICAIONS –
BY NECESSITY –
BUT YES.
HE:
IS –

OF NECESSITY –
INDUBITABLY –
AND:
IRREVOCABLY:
AN:
OVERSOUL.
WHICH MEANS:
THAT:
EVERYONE –
IN HIS –
SPHERE –
HIS:
RANGE –
OF:
PERCEPTION ---
OF:
EXPERIENCE –
IS:
A:
DIRECT:
INCARNATION –
OF:
HIM.
THIS –
OF NECESSITY –
IMPARTS –
A:
I WANT TO SAY:

RESPONSIBILITY –
BUT:
RANDY –
CORRECTS ME.
NO.
WHAT THIS:
OF NECESSITY –
ACCIDENT –
IMPARTS --
IS:
MOTHERHOOD.
RANDY:
IS:
A:
MOTHER.

PART THIRTY-THREE

Nothing progresses.
A doesn't cause B which doesn't cause C.
Everything is created INSTANTANEOUSLY --
Without PRECEDENT.
So forget all your PLANNING --
AND DIAGRAMS.
AND:
LOGIC.
REASONING MIND.
INTELLECT.
EVERY --
THING --
IN --
YOUR --
LIFE --
COMES --
DIRECTLY --
FROM --
YOUR --
MEDITATION PRACTICE.
FROM YOUR:
SINOATRIAL NODE:
FULL BODY THROBBING.
So:

THROW OUT YOUR PLANS.
YOUR REASONING MIND.
AND:
THROB.
……..
If you:
FEEL --
YOUR:
SINOATRIAL NODE --
PULSING --
THROBBING --
AND *STAY THERE* --
LIVE --
THERE --
MAKE YOUR --
THROBBING --
HEART --
YOUR:
HOME --
YOUR:
SANCTUARY --
THEN:
YOU WILL LIVE OUT --
EVERY ROMANTIC FANTASY --
THAT EVER MADE YOU:
BLUSH.
YOU WILL LIVE LIKE A:
ROCKEFELLER.

YOUR --
BODY --
WILL BE THE ENVY --
THE:
DESIRE --
OF BRAD PIT --
ANGELINA JOLIE.
BUT YOU WILL --
NOT --
BE A:
WHORE
YOU WILL BE:
A:
CELIBATE --
ABSTINENT:
SAINT --
WITH EVERY:
HEARTBEAT
WITH EVERY:
PULSE --
OF:
ORGASMIC LIGHT --
REAMING --
YOUR --
NOT EXACTLY --
ACQUIESCING --
NOR REALLY:
FIGHTING IT EITHER:

BODY.
AS YOU GIVE YOUR --
CHILDREN --
FEED --
YOUR CHILDREN --
EXACTLY WHAT THEY NEED --
EXACTLY --
WHAT THEY WERE:
CRAVING.
WHICH IS:
PRECISELY:
THIS.
WHICH IS:
PRECISELY:
YOU.
……..
Our *promise* has always been:
STAY IN YOUR HEART --
AND YOU WILL HAVE:
EVERYTHING YOU WANT.
Our:
TEACHING --
HAS ALWAYS BEEN:
YOU NOW HAVE:
EVERYTHING YOU WANT.
EVERYONE --
ALWAYS GETS --
EXACTLY WHAT THEY WANT.

THAT HAS ALWAYS BEEN TRUE.
AND IT STILL IS.
YOU --
YOUR --
SO-CALLED --
LIE --
OF A:
WORLD --
AND ITS:
CORRUPTIVE --
DISTORTIONS --
SIMPLY --
KEEP YOU FROM SEEING --
THE MOST OBVIOUS THING --
IN THE WORLD.
THE:
MOST --
OBVIOUS --
THING --
IN THE WORLD --
IS THAT:
YOU --
NOW HAVE --
EVERYTHING YOU WANT --
AND EVERYONE --
ALWAYS GETS --
EXACTLY --
WHAT THEY WANT.

AND YOU --
AND YOUR --
WORLD --
AND EVERYONE --
IN --
YOUR WORLD --
IS *PERFECT* --
AND IS--
DOING --
EXACTLY --
WHAT THEY --
NEED TO BE:
DOING.
OUR:
ADVICE:
TO:
ANY OF YOU --
WOULD BE:
JUST:
KEEP DOING --
EXACTLY --
WHAT YOU --
ARE ALREADY --
DOING.
AND OUR HOPE --
IS THAT YOU WILL --
ALSO --
HELP OTHERS --

HELP --
YOUR WORLD --
BY TELLING THEM:
YOU ARE PERFECT.
PLEASE KEEP DOING --
WHAT --
YOU ARE ALREADY:
DOING.
....
Now --
HOW EASY WAS THAT?

PART THIRTY-FOUR

Randy has received a MANTLE.
He has EARNED a mantle.
A MANTLE is being BESTOWED UPON HIM –
Like a ROBE.
He doesn't mind.
He is a good boy.
He does as he is told.
....
Randy cries now when he sees any animal.
He knows that their plight is his plight.
And their plight is:
Well –
Often:
HARROWING.
At night –
When he is sleeping –
He kisses animals on the face –
And says, "I love you" –
As their throats are being slit.
He is happy to –
TUMBLE INTO DEATH WITH THEM.
JUST BECAUSE IT IS SO WONDERFUL –
JUST TO BE WITH THEM.
And he wants to –

HELP THEM.
They are his children.

....

Randy doesn't cry –
So readily –
When he looks –
At people.
They are his:
CHILDEN –
NONETHELESS –
But mostly what he sees is:
WHO HE USED TO BE WHEN HE WAS HUMAN.
WHO HE USED TO BE WHEN HE WAS EGO.
RANDY IS NO LONGER EGO.
HE IS NO LONGER HUMAN.
HUMAN WAS A CHRYSALIS –
AND NOW *HIS:*
LIES –
LIFELESS –
ON THE GROUND.
NO MORE PITIABLE –
THAN A BROWN LEAF.
OR AN EMPTY:
COCOON.

,,,,,,,

Randy is EVERYONE.
And:
EVERYTHING.

But:

ON SCALE.

His world is NOT a:

FUNHOUSE MIRROR –

But it is a mirror –

TO SCALE.

He sees –

ACCURATELY –

WHO AND WHAT HE IS –

IN PROPORTION.

Of course all beings are:

HOLOGRAPHIC of each other.

EACH CONTAINS THE ALL.

That is why there can be no SAINTS or SINNERS.

Point to any one of you and say, "HE IS THE DEVIL" –

And I will point to the SAME PERSON and say:

"THIS ONE IS THE:

GODHEAD ITSELF."

THE ONLY ONE WHO IS A DEVIL IS THE ONE POINTING THEIR FINGER AND SAYING:

"THAT ONE IS A DEVIL."

A HOLOGRAM –

CAN'T GET AWAY FROM ITSELF.

We have called this the:

CURSE OF BEING ALL THAT IS.

But it is not a curse.

AT ALL.

NOT WHEN YOU SEE THAT:

EVERY ONE OF THESE –

"FOUL BEINGS" –
IS ACTUALLY –
CATEGORICALLY –
INCONTROVERTIBLY –
AND *BY DEFINITION:*
THE MOST –
PRECIOUS –
DARLING –
SWEETHEART –
BELOVED –
SOULMATE:
LOVE OF YOUR LIFE --
WHO –
Again –
BY DEFINITION –
CAN:
DO NO WRONG.
You:
SADLY –
ARE:
IN LOVE.
……..
Don't forget –
AND I DO MEAN TO BOLSTER YOU HERE –
YOU ARE NOT SO FAR REMOVED FROM THE APES.
YOU:
ARE:

STILL:
ANIMAL.
ANIMALS –
ARE THE:
BEST PART –
OF YOU.
Forget about human.
That is all:
EGOIC NONSENSE.
We have been arguing all along that:
HUMANITY NEVER EXISTED.
It is a clever:
VIDEO GAME.
There was a discussion recently –
And I will repeat it.
In Plato's *Allegory of the Cave* –
A group of people are chained up in a cave –
IMMOBILIZED.
They face the BACK WALL OF THE CAVE –
Upon which they view:
MOVING SHADOWS.
Because this is all they have –
EVER SEEN –
Of course –
THEY THINK THESE SHADOWS ARE REAL.
SHADOWS:
HERE:
REFER TO:
EVERYTHING:

YOU CONSIDER TO BE:

PHYSICAL REALITY.

Please join the *GROWING SWELL* OF CONTEMPORARY PHYSICISTS –

WHO WILL –

ONE AND ALL –

TELL YOU --

THAT:

PHYSICAL REALITY:

DOES:

NOT:

EXIST.

And now I will explain.

EYES:

SEE SHADOWS.

EARS:

HEAR SHADOWS.

HANDS:

TOUCH SHADOWS.

TONGUES:

TASTE SHADOWS.

NOSES:

SMELL SHADOWS.

HEARTS:

SEE:

LIGHT.

HEARTS:

SEE:

FIRE DIRECTLY.

HEARTS:
SEE:
ONLY:
GODHEAD LIGHT –
BECAUSE YOU CAN ONLY:
SEE WHAT YOU ARE.
And please let that sink in:
YOU CAN ONLY SEE:
WHAT YOU ARE.
....
Do you know what the heart sees when it looks at a shadow?
THE LIGHT THAT CASTS THAT SHADOW.
AND THAT IS WHY:
RANDY HAS RECEIVED –
EARNED –
BEEN BESTOWED:
THIS MANTLE.
PRECISELY BECAUSE:
RANDY:
CAN LOOK NOW –
AT THE:
VILEST OF SHADOWS –
AND SEE:
ONLY:
LIGHT.

PART THIRTY-FIVE

You don't get to choose the life you have.

You don't get to choose the SELF you have.

You do not get to choose who your friends are.

You do not get to choose what your occupation will be.

You do not get to choose whether you will have a lover.

Or who your lover will be.

Or who you will fall in love with.

Or what you will have for breakfast.

You do not get to choose whether you will have sex.

Or what kind of sex you will have.

You do not get to choose whether you will be enlightened.

You do not get to choose what planet you will be on.

Or if you will be incarnated or not.

You do not choose when you will be born.

Or when:

Or *HOW:*

You will die.

You do not choose what you eat.

Or what you wear.

Or how wealthy you will be.

Or whether you live in poverty.

Or whether you'll end up sleeping on the sidewalk.

Or whether you'll get a Ph.D.

Or move to Los Angeles and become famous.

Or whether you will get a Ph.D. and then MEET someone who moved to Los Angeles and became famous.

You do not get to choose what you will say.

Or what you will do.

On any given day.

Or any given moment.

Is there anything you –

DO –

Get to choose?

Frankly?

Honestly?

NO.

....

There is no "inside" or "outside."

There is no physical or nonphysical.

There is no alive or dead.

There is no planet revolving around the sun.

You do not die –

EVER.

There is no death.

There is no permanence.

There is no –

FREE WILL.

No choice,

At all.

....

You need to be alone more.

There is something happening in your life.

It started a long time ago.

Epochs, eons ago.

But there has been an –

INCREASING ACCERATION –

Rather suddenly it seems.

Let's not say "world."

Let's not say "person."

Let's call it:

THIS THIING THAT YOU ARE.

This:

AMALGAMATION.

This:

INTERPENETRATING –

LIKE A WOVEN CLOTH –

INNER GALAXY AND OUTER GALAXY –

BROAD BRUSH STROKE –

VISTA –

YAWNING CANYON –

MULTIPLE INTERMINGLING TERRAINS –

ALL PAST PROBALITIES AND ALL FUTURE PROBABILITIES –

NOT EVEN CONTRADICTING EACH OTHER –

BUT:

PROLIFERATING OFF EACH OTHER –

PROPAGATING OFF EACH OTHER.

LIKE YOU CAN'T STOP HAVING SEX EVEN IF YOU WANTED TO.

....

You really can't stop having sex even if you want to.

EVEN IF YOU HAVEN'T HAD A LOVER –

OR AN ORGASM –
IN YEARS –
YOUR SEXUALITY –
YOUR:
EROTIC NATURE –
DOES NOT STOP LOOMING --
SURGING –
URGING –
SPLURGING –
IN EACH AND EVERY ONE OF THESE "WORLDS" –
WHICH DO IN FACT COMPRISE –
"YOUR" –
"WORLD."
....
I said you have no CHOICE.
This NEW PARADIGM will look:
INSANE –
From the OLD PARADIGM.
JUST AS THE OLD PARADIGM –
APPEARS:
PITIABLE –
TO THE NEW ONE.
Every "TRUTH" you've ever had –
Believed –
CHERISHED –
Has been:
RIPPED AWAY.
DISPROVEN.
EXPOSED.

DISINTEGRATED BEFORE YOUR EYES –
JUST AS YOUR:
WORLD –
HAS DISINTEGRATED.
INCREASINGLY:
PEOPLE WILL ANNOY YOU.
EVEN THE ONES YOU LOVE THE MOST –
WILL ANNOY YOU.
YOU WILL FIND IT –
NEARLY IMPOSSIBLE –
AND:
INCREASINGLY:
EXHAUSTING –
UNTENABLE –
UNDESIRABLE –
TO BE IN THE SAME ROOM AS THEM FOR FIVE MINUTES.
You LOVE THEM –
All the same.
But a:
BRIEF –
ANONYMOUS –
POLITELY AVOIDANT –
TEXT –
WILL INCREASINGLY –
AND EVENTUALLY ALTOGETHER –
REPLACE –
ALL THE:
"HANGING OUT" –

AND HOURS LONG –
INTIMATE –
SOUL SHARING –
GAZING INTO EACH OTHER'S EYES –
CONVERSATIONS –
There used to be.
That just isn't where the:
MAGIC –
Is, anymore.
THE PEOPLE IN YOUR LIFE –
WILL STILL BE IN YOUR LIFE –
BUT THEY WILL BE LIKE:
SQUIRRELS IN YOUR YARD –
CATTLE IN YOUR FIELDS –
BIRDS IN YOUR TREES –
STARS IN YOUR SKIES.
You *APPRECIATE* them –
As an:
ORANGE AND PINK SUNSET –
OR A WISTFUL –
GAZE –
AT THE MOON.
They will evoke the:
PATHOS –
MAYBE EVEN TEARFUL –
MEMORY –
OF AN OLD LOVE.
Like:
"GOOD TO SEE YOU."

A:
BRIEF –
HUG –
AND "HOW HAVE YOU BEEN?"
BUT YOU NOTICE YOU'RE ALREADY –
WALKING AWAY –
BEFORE YOU EVEN:
OPEN YOUR MOUTH.
AND WHEN THEY ARE GONE –
YOU:
SIGH:
DEEPLY.
THEY ARE JUST --
NOT:
WHERE THE MAGIC IS:
ANYMORE.
....
No.
The MAGIC –
Is in the:
MONOLITHIC –
INTELLIGENT –
ALWAYS MORPHING –
AMALGAMATION.
MULTIPLE TERRAINS –
INTERPENETRATING AND INTERMINGLING WITH ITSELF –
LIKE IT HAS A:
PLAN.

OR AT LEAST A:
STRUCTURAL INTEGRITY –
DNA –
A:
BLUEPRINT –
LIKE ANY:
ACORN –
DOES.
....
You are starting to:
GRASP –
THAT THIS:
INTELLIGENT –
SENTIENT --
AMALGAMATION –
OF INTERPENETRATING INTEMIGLING TERRAINS –
MORPHING AND –
FRACTALING ENDLESSLY –
BOTH INSIDE AND OUTSIDE ITSELF –
IS AN:
INDEPENDENT –
AND AS FAR AS YOU CAN TELL:
NEW –
AND NEVER SEEN BEFORE –
ORGANISM.
SPECIES.
DEVOURING –
ALL THE PRIOR –
SPECIES –

IN ITS WAKE.
MAKING THEM:
THE CELLS –
AND ATOMS –
OF ITS OWN:
BODY.
ANATOMY.
LIKE A PARSITIC:
SYMBIOTE.
AND YOU REALIZE –
NOT EXACTLY WITH:
ALARM –
OR:
DISTRESS –
THAT THIS:
PARASITIC SYMBIOTE –
HAS ALSO –
IN FACT –
DEVOURED:
YOU.
....
IT HAS ALSO –
IN FACT:
DEVOURED –
YOUR WORLD –
AND EVERYONE –
AND EVERYTHING –
IN IT.
IT HAS DEVOURED YOUR:

SOLAR SYSTEM.
YOUR GALAXY.
RANDY JUST DISCOVERED –
THAT YOUR GALAXY –
ALONG WITH:
COUNTLESS OTHER NEIGHBORING GALAXIES –
ARE IN FACT –
REVOLGING AROUND A:
SINGLE BLACK HOLE –
THAT YOUR PHYSICISTS –
CAN ONLY NOW HYPOTHESIZE.
BUT YOU *KNOW* –
THAT THIS:
INTELLIGENT –
SENTIENT
AMALGAMATION --
OF:
INTERPENETRATING INTERMINGLING TERRAINS –
HAS DEVOURED –
EVEN THIS:
GALAXY OF GALAXIES.
AND –
PRESUMABLY:
THE GALAXY OF GALAXIES OF GALAXIES –
BEYOND THAT.
AND BEYOND THAT.
AND BEYOND THAT.
....
SINCE BEING DEVOURED –

YOU DON'T QUITE FEEL LIKE YOURSELF.
YOU ARE FLOATING IN AN:
EXPANSE OF LIGHT.
FOR THAT DOES SEEM TO BE –
WHAT THIS NEW ORGANISM:
IS.
AN EXPANSE OF:
INTELLIGENT:
LIGHT.
YOUR *WILL* –
HAS BEEN EXPUNGED.
AS IF SURGICALLY.
CHOICE HAS BECOME –
NOT ONLY:
IMPOSSIBLE –
BUT IRRELEVANT.
MEANINGLESS.
OBSOLETE.
LIKE SOMETHING –
CAVEMEN –
ONCE DID.
The:
SYMBOSIS –
Is:
TWO WAY.
BIDIRECTIONAL.
BECAUSE –
ONE OF THE FIRST THINGS YOU NOTICE –
IS THAT YOU ARE:

NOW:
OMNISCIENT.
AND:
HAPPY.
HELL –
YOU COULD BE:
JESUS –
OR THE BUDDHA –
OR QUAN YIN –
OR EVEN:
THE GODHEAD –
ITSELF.
YOU COULD –
AND YOU:
ARE.
ESPECIALLY SINCE YOUR:
BODY –
IDENTIY –
WORLD –
BRAIN –
HEART --
GOT:
OBLIVIATED –
DESOLVED –
SWALLOWED –
BY:
LIGHT.
....
YOU ARE A:

CELL –
AN:
ATOM –
IN THS MASSIVE –
GARGANTUA.
Some ENZYME –
MUST HAVE –
DISSOLVED –
YOUR WILL –
YOUR:
MIND.
SURPRISINGLY –
YOU:
DON'T:
MISS:
IT.
YOU FEEL LIKE A:
VENTRILOQUIST'S –
DUMMY.
WITH A:
HAND –
UP –
YOUR ASS.
AND YOU:
NOTICE –
THAT YOU:
LIKE IT.
A LOT.
YOU FEEL LIKE YOU ARE –

WITNESSING –
LIVING –
THE:
GREATEST STORY EVER TOLD.
AND YOU:
LAUGH –
WHEN IT HITS YOU –
THAT:
YOU:
YOUR *NEW* –
YOU –
IS A –
WHOLE LOT –
MORE INTERESTING –
THAN JESUS –
EVER WAS.
FOR YOU HAVE:
BEHELD –
YOU ARE:
WATCHING –
BOTH –
YOU –
AND THIS:
MASSIVE –
IRRESTIBLE –
INTELLIGENT –
SENTIENT –
AMALGAMATION –
OF:

INTERPENETRATING INTERMINGLING TERRAINS –
GLEEFULLY –
TUMBLING –
HEAD OVER HEELS –
UNRESERVEDLY –
UNABASHEDLY –
IN LOVE –
WITH EACH OTHER.
WHO KNEW –
THAT YOUR NEXT:
EVOLUTIONARY –
LEAP –
WOULD BE A:
MARRIAGE VOW.

PART THIRTY-SIX

Randy has arrived.
He is in love.
He is a #1 best selling author.
He is financially secure for life.
He owns a house --
IN THE MOST BEAUTIFUL PLACE IN THE WORLD.
He shares his soul with a cat.
HE SHARES A SOUL WITH MANY PEOPLE.
AND ANIMALS.
AND TREES.
AND FLOWERS.
AND ROCKS.
AND INSECTS.
AND MOUNTAINS.
AND OCEANS.
AND STARS.
DO YOU KNOW --
THAT PLACE --
BEHIND THE SCENES --
BEHIND --
IT ALL --
THAT:
ORCHESTRATES THINGS?
CHOREOGRAPHS THINGS?

PULLS THE STRINGS?

Well:

THAT IS WHERE RANDY LIVES NOW.

Randy ORCHESTRATES.

He CHOREOGRAPHS.

He:

PULLS THE STRINGS.

If you asked him to --

CREATE --

Something for you --

He'd say:

I ALREADY:

HAVE.

I ALREADY:

AM.

THE QUESTION IS:

"DO YOU LIKE IT?"

Or *MORE TO THE POINT:*

"HAVE YOU --

NOTICED --

IT."

BECAUSE:

IT'S RIGHT:

IN FRONT:

OF YOUR:

FACE.

....

They say LIFE DOESN'T COME WITH AN INSTRUCTION MANUAL --

But --

THAT ISN'T TRUE.

WHAT DO YOU THINK DNA IS?

Each cell in your body is:

OMNISCIENT.

So is each:

ATOM.

ALL YOU HAVE TO DO IS:

READ THE CELLS --

AND ATOMS --

OF YOUR BODY --

LIKE YOU WERE --

READING AN:

ENCYCLOPEDIA --

OR:

THE AKASHIC RECORDS.

It is a bit:

TIME INTENSIVE.

But once you DO IT --

AND LEARN HOW TO DO IT ON A REGULAR BASIS --

Then you are:

OMNISCIENT.

And:

CAN ACT ACCORDINGLY.

You will --

ALWAYS KNOW WHAT TO DO.

Or:

NOT DO.

With OMNISCIENCE --
Comes a kind of:
GRACE.
An:
UNCONSCIOUS GRACE.
Randy never wonders what he should DO --
Because:
HE'S ALREADY DOING IT.
Life becomes:
VERY EASY.
In fact:
ONCE YOU BECOME:
OMNISCIENT --
YOU NEVER HAVE TO:
DO:
ANYTHING --
EVER AGAIN.
IT IS --
ALL --
DONE --
FOR YOU.
WHEN YOU BECOME:
OMNISCIENT --
"WORLD" --
Takes on a:
NEW DEFINITION.
"WORLD" --
IS NOW --

DEFINED --
AS:
YOU -
GETTING --
EVERYTHING --
YOU --
WANT.
When you are:
OMNISCIENT --
You END UP --
Saying:
THANK YOU --
A LOT.
TO YOURSELF.
You STAND IN FRONT OF A MIRROR --
OFTEN --
SAYING:
"YOU --
ARE --
THE --
MOST BEAUTIFUL--
THING --
I HAVE EVER --
SEEN."
Of course you say the same thing --
To every:
FLOWER --
STAR --

COW --
PERSON --
YOU SEE.
BECAUSE:
THAT --
IS THE:
MIRROR --
WE'RE --
TALKING ABOUT.
……..
Randy's JUNGIAN ANALYST --
Often asked him:
"IF I WAS FROM MARS --
AND DIDN'T KNOW --
WHAT YOU WERE --
TALKING ABOUT --
HOW WOULD YOU:
EXPLAIN IT?"
Ahhh...
The DEADLINESS of:
LABELS.
The DEADLINESS of:
WORDS --
In general.
How would you describe:
LOVE?
Or:
LOVER?

Or:

LIFE?

Or:

WORLD?

Or:

JOY?

Or:

TIME?

Or:

RAPTURE?

Or:

MEANING?

Or:

PURPOSE?

Or:

SATISFACTION?

And --

NOW --

IMAGINE --

THIS:

EXTRATERRESTRIAL --

TRYING --

TO:

EXPLAIN --

TO:

YOU --

SOMETHING THAT --

YOU --

HAD NO FRAME OF REFERENCE --
FOR.
BECAUSE:
THAT'S WHAT WE'RE TALKING ABOUT.
Do you know that there is:
An *EXTRATERRESTRIAL* --
LIVING --
INSIDE ALL OF YOU?
That just means:
THE PART
OF YOU --
THAT IS NOT:
"OF THIS WORLD."
I am talking about your:
OBSERVER SELF.
Your:
WITNESS.
The:
GREAT I AM.
The:
EYE IN THE SKY.
The:
YOU OF *YOU.*
I am talking about your:
DREAMING SELF.
I am talking about:
WHO YOU ARE WHEN YOU DREAM.
Which is the same:

YOU --
As:
WHO YOU ARE WHEN YOU *DIE.*
You see:
MARS --
ISN'T AS --
FAR AWAY --
AS YOU THOUGHT IT WAS.
....
You will know you have ARRIVED --
When you:
HAVE EVERYTHING YOU WANT --
AND *KNOW* --
THAT YOU ALWAYS WILL.
You will know that you have ARRIVED --
WHEN YOU --
FLIP TO:
AUTOMATIC PILOT --
AND:
ALL OF YOUR DREAMS --
COME TRUE --
IN EVERY MOMENT --
WITHOUT:
YOU --
HAVING TO LIFT A FINGER --
OR EVEN:
GIVE IT:
A THOUGHT.

In fact:
YOU WILL KNOW YOU HAVE ARRIVED --
WHEN YOU:
NO LONGER --
HAVE --
THOUGHT.
OR:
DESIRE --
OR:
ANY:
URGE --
FOR ANYTHING --
TO BE --
ANYTHING DIFFERENT --
FROM HOW IT:
ALREADY IS.
You will NOTICE:
You have just STEPPED INTO:
HYPERSPACE.
The:
QUANTUM UNIVERSE.
Once you have:
LOST ALL DESIRE --
You will DISCOVER --
That you --
Do --
In fact --
HAVE --

EVERYTHING YOU WANT.
But it WILL NOT BE --
That you are:
SETTLING FOR LESS.
And this is where --
It will feel as though --
SOMEONE --
Has SLIPPED YOU A TAB OF LSD.
Because the UNDENIABLE --
INDISPUTABLE --
TRUTH --
Is that:
WHAT --
LIFE --
DELIVERS TO YOU --
ON A:
SILVER PLATTER --
ON A:
CONVEYOR BELT --
CONTINUOUSLY --
CEASELESSLY –
IN EVERY INSTANT --
IS:
EXPONENTIALLY --
QUANTUMLY --
BEYOND YOUR --
WILDEST --
DREAMS.

YOU --
KNOW --
THAT YOU HAVE --
INADVERTENTLY --
TUMBLED --
INTO A:
BLACK HOLE --
AND ARE NOW --
IN AN ENTIRELY DIFFERENT --
UNIVERSE --
WITH ALTOGETHER --
UNRECOGNIZABLE --
LAWS OF PHYSICS.
BECAUSE THE:
SILLIEST --
RANDOMEST --
MOST:
OUTRAGEOUS --
MIRACLE --
(BECAUSE --
THAT IS ABSOLUTELY --
WHAT THEY ARE) --
IS:
LIGHT YEARS --
BEYOND --
ANYTHING --
YOU EVER:
DARED TO DREAM.

....

This new SPECIES --

FOR THAT IS WHAT WE ARE TALKING ABOUT --

Could be called:

THEY WHO GET EVERYTHING THEY WANT ALL THE TIME WITHOUT LIFTING A FINGER OR EVEN GIVING IT A THOUGHT.

Yes we are talking about:

CARS.

And:

HOUSES.

And:

MORE MONEY THAN YOU KNOW WHAT TO DO WITH.

And:

LOVERS.

And:

STATUS.

And:

A HEALTHY RADIANT SEXY SINGING BODY.

BUT:

WE ARE ALSO TALKING ABOUT:

THE:

WILDEST DREAMS --

OF THAT:

EXTRATERRESTRIAL --

WITHIN YOU.

The DREAMING YOU.

The:

DEAD YOU.
The:
WATCHING YOU.
THE:
GOD:
YOU.
You will get to know --
YOU WILL GET TO:
RELISH --
SAVOR --
EXULT IN --
All the --
UNBEARABLE --
ORGASMIC --
PLEASURES --
THAT ARE THE --
WILDEST DREAMS --
OF ALL THESE:
EXTRATERRESTRIAL --
YOUS.
ALL OF THESE:
GOD YOUS.
YOU START TO:
COMPREHEND --
THAT YOU MAY NOT --
SURVIVE --
THIS:
CONTINUOUS ONSLAUGHT --

OF GALAXY EXPLODING:
ORGASMS.
BUT THEN YOU:
LAUGH --
WHEN IT --
HITS YOU --
THAT IT:
DOESN'T MATTER --
ONE --
LITTLE --
BIT.
BECAUSE YOU NOW --
ARE:
THROUGH AND THROUGH:
IMMORTAL.

PART THIRTY-SEVEN

Randy's heart is a STAR.
He sees other stars, and admires --
And says hello --
Or whatever.
But he has his own:
LIGHT.
And his own:
ORBIT.
AS DO THEY --
Of course.
Randy is a:
BRIGHT STAR.
But one of billions --
TRILLIONS --
And of course --
TRILLIONS OF TRILLIONS OF TRILLIONS --
Beyond that.
There is no:
HUBRIS.
Nor is there:
INSECURITY.
Or:
EVEN IF THERE IS --
That:

HUBRIS --
That:
INSECURITY --
SHINES BRIGHT AS THE SUN.
Do you know what a star sees --
When it looks into a mirror?
LIGHT.
Do you know what a star sees --
WHEN IT LOOKS INTO:
THE *MIRROR OF ITS WORLD?*
TRILLIONS OF TRILLIONS OF TRILLIONS OF:
POINTS OF LIGHT.
SHINING BACK.

....

You don't navigate Life.
LIFE --
NAVIGATES --
YOU.
What I mean is:
LIFE --
PUSHES --
YOU --
AROUND.
You are all:
ELECTRIC.
MAGNETIC.
Sometimes you will:
INVOLUNTARILY --

SMASH --
COLLIDE -
GET:
SUCKED INTO --
EACH OTHER.
Other times:
You will --
KNOCK EACH OTHER OUT OF THE GALAXY --
LIKE A HOME RUN.
There's really --
NOTHING YOU CAN DO ABOUT IT --
Either way.
No blame --
No --
APOLOGIES --
Are called for.
A period of:
LICKING ONE'S WOUNDS --
Or:
DIMMING ONE'S LIGHT --
Is perfectly understandable.
No blame --
Or apologies --
Necessary there --
Either.
DEITIES --
HAVE DIGNITY --
NO MATTER WHAT THEY DO.

EVEN:
AT THEIR:
VILEST.
A SUN:
CAN'T STOP:
SHINING.
....
You can't really --
GET AWAY FROM YOURSELF.
Nor would you:
WANT TO.
YOU:
ARE:
WONDERFUL.
YOU KNOW IT.
EVERYONE KNOWS IT.
No charge --
OR *CRIME* --
COULD:
CHALLENGE --
OR:
INVALIDATE:
THAT.
Not only have you achieved:
IMMORTALITY.
You have achieved:
SINLESSNESS.
AND SO:

HAS EVERYONE ELSE.

....

You still:

LOOK INTO EACH OTHER'S:

EYES --

AND WANT TO:

FLEE --

OR:

FIGHT.

WANT TO:

KILL --

OR:

WANT:

TO:

BE:

KILLED.

You wonder:

Do immortals:

KILL --

INSTEAD OF:

FUCK?

....

Take the:

FEAR --

Of death away --

Take the:

SIN --

Of death away --

And:

BOY OH BOY OH BOY!

You are in a:

NEW:
PLAYING FIELD.

The urge to:

HELP --

Is OBSOLETE --

Because NOBODY --

NEEDS ANY.

So the:

GOLDEN RULE:

BECOMES:

KILL --

AS YOU WOULD LIKE TO BE:

KILLED.

PART THIRTY-EIGHT

We just told Randy:
YOUR HAND IS ON THE SPIGOT.
He can't control WHAT comes out of it.
But he can control:
HOW --
HOW MUCH --
And:
HOW FAST.
In case you were wondering --
We DID EMPHASIZE:
MORE IS NOT BETTER.
FASTER IS NOT BETTER.
In case you're wondering --
WHAT EXACTLY HE DOES:
He LIES DOWN.
On back or sides, it doesn't matter.
He:
ENTERS HIS HEART --
And FINDS --
The SINOATRIAL NODE --
Which:
RHYTHMICALLY --
FIRES --
THE ELECTRICAL --

SPARK OF LIFE --
THAT BEATS YOUR HEART.
Secondarily --
He:
FEELS:
RELISHES IN --
The:
HYPNOTIC:
FULL BODY THROB.
It is a LOVELY --
And THOROUGHLY PLEASANT --
PRACTICE.
He does this EVERY AFTERNOON --
From 2 - 7:00 --
RELIGIOUSLY.
And also:
ANY OTHER TIME OF THE DAY OR NIGHT --
HE GETS THE CHANCE.
Our first TEACHING to him --
When he was twenty-one --
Was:
STAY IN YOUR HEART --
AND YOU WILL HAVE EVERYTHING YOU WANT.
That is as true now --
As it was then.
....
Initially --
He thought he would be praying for Gavin.
Gavin is Randy's:

MAN FRIEND.

MENTOR.

PROTEGE.

HELPMATE.

Gavin is having bad allergies and Randy thought he would help.

Randy is *LEARNING* --

OF COURSE.

LOOK AT WHO HE HANGS OUT WITH!

Years ago we taught him a variation on the:

PATANJALI PRAYER --

Which was a POWERHOUSE --

MIRACLE PRODUCER.

Compared to that --

This new technique is a:

SUPER NOVA.

You see --

You're not:

FIXING --

ANYTHING.

REALITY GETS --

RECREATED --

COUNTLESS TIMES --

EVERY INSTANT.

So fast you can't SEE IT --

But you can *FEEL IT*.

LIKE A MACHINE GUN.

SO:

YOU DON'T:

"FIX" --
The current reality.
You CREATE --
A *NEW ONE.*
WHICH ISN'T AS HARD AS IT MIGHT SEEM --
BECAUSE:
YOU'RE DOING IT ANYWAY.
NOW --
You're just bringing your:
AWARENESS.
Your OMNISCIENCE.
Your LOVE.
Your WONDER.
Your:
JOY.
AND OURS.
You see:
NOW --
YOU ARE CONNECTED --
TO THE:
HIGHER ECHELONS --
OF:
WHO YOU ARE.
We must comment here:
The almost:
FANATICAL --
LOVE --
RANDY HAS --

FOR US --
AND FOR LIFE --
AND FOR GAVIN:
IS HIS:
ROCKET FUEL.
....
The CHOREOGRAPHER here --
Is CLEVER BEYOND COMPREHENSION.
We know that REALITY --
GENERALLY --
Feels like:
JUST A TAD --
TOO MUCH.
It is DESIGNED that way --
Of course.
This:
CURRICULUM DESIGNER --
KNOWS WHAT YOU NEED --
SO MUCH MORE PRECISELY --
THAN YOU POSSIBLY COULD.
You will learn --
AS RANDY HAS --
THAT THE WHOLE --
MOTIVE --
DRIVING THIS:
INFINITE --
HIERARCHY OF ECHELONS --
IS:

LOVE.
THIS INCLUDES:
LOVE OF HATE.
LOVE OF VIOLENCE.
THAT'S --
HOW POWERFUL --
A *TSUNAMI* --
OF LOVE --
WE'RE TALKING ABOUT.
IT IS THE LOVE --
OF KALI.
EVERYTHING YOU CHERISH --
WILL BE:
RIPPED AWAY --
IN A FIREY --
MAELESTROM --
OF APOCALYPTIC --
MISERY.
YOU CAN'T GET AWAY FROM THAT.
YOU:
JUST:
CAN'T.
That has been the theme of Randy's --
ENTIRE LIFE.
Randy's LIFE --
Has been:
ONE LONG CONTINUOUS:
APOCALYPSE.

That is BECAUSE:
LIFE --
IS ONE LONG CONTINUOUS:
APOCALYPSE.
I mentioned the *MACHINE GUN* --
Of CONTINUOUS RECREATION.
The LOGICAL --
And NECESSARY --
COROLLARY --
COUNTERPART --
Is that:
COUNTLESS TIMES --
EVERY INSTANT --
YOUR ENTIRE --
PHYSICAL UNIVERSE --
MUST BE:
DESTROYED.
In short:
YOU HAVE TO GET --
REALLY GOOD --
AT:
DYING.
AND LOSING --
EVERYTHING --
YOU CHERISH.
....
OK.
Think about it.

Imagine that you HAD --
EVERYTHING YOU EVER WANTED --
(Which ironically --
As you will learn --
You *ALREADY DO).*
STILL --
AND ALL:
YOU WOULD NOT:
BE:
HAPPY.
You see:
OMNISCIENCE --
IS NOT --
OPTIONAL.
YOU --
HAVE TO --
UNDERSTAND --
WHO --
YOU ARE.
AND YOU HAVE TO --
UNDERSTAND --
HOW --
REALITY --
WORKS.
Not only do you HAVE TO.
You NEED TO.
And you:
WANT TO.

We KNOW THIS:
BECAUSE:
WE --
ARE --
YOU.
IT IS NOT ARROGANCE TO SAY --
THAT WE KNOW YOU --
BETTER THAN YOU --
KNOW YOURSELVES.
WE CERTAINLY:
LOVE YOU --
MORE --
THAN YOU LOVE --
YOURSELVES.
You're just going to have to:
TRUST US --
ON THIS ONE.
YOU HAVE ALL --
SIGNED UP --
TO BECOME:
UNIVERSE CREATORS.
Some of you even aspire to be:
MULTIVERSE/OMNIVERSE/ANTIVERSE --
CREATORS.
THE SKY IS THE LIMIT --
BUT REMEMBER:
MORE IS NOT BETTER.
BETTER TO:

DO WHAT YOU DO.
AND BE AMAZED --
BY WHAT YOU DO.
AND BE AMAZED --
BY THE *RESULTS* --
OF WHAT YOU DO.
AND ALSO:
BE AMAZED:
BY WHAT HAPPENS TO YOU --
THAT HAS NOTHING TO DO WITH --
WHAT YOU DID.
YOU ARE GOING TO HAVE TO ACCEPT THE FACT --
THAT:
WE LOVE YOU --
MORE THAN YOU --
COULD POSSIBLY --
COMPREHEND.

PART THIRTY-NINE

There is a CONVEYOR BELT --
Bringing you GIFTS --
On SILVER PLATTERS --
CONTINUOUSLY.
Randy knows this --
Because we have told him --
And because he has EXPERIENCED IT.
He experiences this:
EVERY DAY --
MOMENT BY MOMENT.
This IMAGE --
Gets *REALLY INTERESTING* --
When you START TO WONDER:
WHO IS SENDING THESE GIFTS --
DIRECTLY TO:
YOU?
SOMEONE:
LOVES YOU:
THAT MUCH.
....
If you think in terms of:
GOD --
You AREN'T WRONG --
But you're MISSING THE POINT.

OF COURSE YOU'LL SEE A:
PATTERN --
TO THESE GIFTS.
THEMES.
MOTIFS, if you will.
And if you look still more CLOSELY --
And CAREFULLY --
You may begin to discern:
HIGHLY STRUCTURED:
CURRICULA.
Some of these courses, classrooms --
Are of such:
HIGHLY COMPLEX --
MIND BOGGLING --
INTELLECTUAL --
ALMOST COMPUTER-LIKE:
RIGOR --
THAT YOU BEGIN TO SUSPECT --
IF NOT FOUL PLAY --
THEN:
EXTRATERRESTRIAL ORIGINS.
If you're thinking --
LITTLE GREEN MEN --
You AREN'T WRONG.
But you are:
MISSING THE POINT.
....
Last year --

When Randy was writing *HOLY LOVE* --
He met a young man named PUMA.
They hiked.
And talked for hours.
Puma liked to cook for Randy.
Randy babysat Puma's cat.
Puma gave Randy a key to his house, which he still has.
Puma is clearly --
Not just a LIFELONG FRIEND --
But an:
EONS-LONG SOULMATE.
One day --
After a LONG HIKE --
And a BEAUTIFUL DAY TOGETHER --
THAT NIGHT --
Randy had a HARD-ON --
That KEPT HIM AWAKE --
ALL NIGHT LONG.
ENTIRELY UNDERSTANDABLY --
Randy heard wedding bells.
He was --
ENTIRELY UNDERSTANDABLY --
MISSING THE POINT.
....
Last year Randy met a:
GOD ON EARTH.
His name is GAVIN DILLARD.
They met --

And Gavin offered to buy a HOUSE --
For the two of them to live in.
Randy explained --
That he already had a house --
And elderly parents to care for.
But this:
COSMIC COLLISION --
Continued to ROCK THEM --
For the better part of a year.
GONADS WERE STIRRED.
But more than that:
HEARTS.
And SOULS.
They wrote a BOOK TOGETHER --
Telling their WONDROUS TALE --
And its FAR-REACHING --
COSMIC IMPLICATIONS.
What a *WONDROUS GIFT* --
On a *WONDROUS PLATTER* --
ALL OF THAT WAS!
It took BOTH THEIR --
BREATHS AWAY.
And sent them:
QUITE CAREENING.
But they CAUGHT THEMSELVES.
More truly:
LIFE CAUGHT THEM.
More SWEETLY:

LIFE:
TAPPED THEM ON THE SHOULDER --
And WHISPERED:
"YOU NEED TO:
OPEN YOUR HANDS --
AND HEARTS --
AND LET GO OF --
WHAT YOU'VE BEEN:
HOLDING ONTO --
IN ORDER TO:
RECEIVE --
THE NEXT PLATTER --
THAT IS EVEN NOW --
APPEARING OVER THE HORIZON."

....

Randy and Gavin --
Will remain:
EONS-LONG SOULMATES.
SUCH BONDS ARE --
BY DEFINITION:
ETERNAL.
Broken hearts are --
From GOD'S POINT OF VIEW --
From the ETS' POINT OF VIEW --
And ultimately --
If you are HONEST --
From *YOUR* POINT OF VIEW --
(And now --

PERHAPS --
You have figured out WHO --
Has been SENDING YOU THESE --
GIFTS ON SILVER PLATES.
This GOD --
These ETS --
This YOU --
THIS:
YOUER YOU) --
But yes.
If you are HONEST.
YOU WILL SEE.
HOW SILLY.
BROKEN HEARTS ARE.
WHEN YOU ARE --
LITERALLY --
DROWNING --
IN AN:
OCEAN OF LOVE.
AND:
GIFTS --
KEEP ARRIVING --
WITH YOUR NAME ON THEM --
CONTINUOUSLY.
AND --
SOMEONE:
KEEPS TAPPING YOUR:

SHOULDER:
AND WHISPERING:
SCRIPTURAL:
SWEET NOTHINGS:
IN YOUR EAR.
BOTH GAVIN'S --
AND RANDY'S --
EARS --
ARE NOW HEARING:
"BOW DEEPLY.
TO EACH OTHER.
AND SMILE --
BECAUSE YOU CAN'T HELP IT.
AND KNOW:
THAT WHAT YOU HAD --
AND HAVE --
IS:
ABSOLUTELY:
FOREVER."

PART FORTY

Free will operates on the physical
And astral levels.
THERE IS NO FREE WILL ON
THE CAUSAL PLANE.
There is no need.
The whole CONCEPT is obsolete.
On the CAUSAL plane there is no:
"Person in the world."
There is just:
YOU.
And YOU --
ARE --
THE WORLD.
THE OUTSIDE --
IS THE INSIDE --
AND:
VICE VERSA.
On the CAUSAL PLANE --
You are the:
WATCHER --
NOT --
THE DOER.
There IS no "doer" on the causal plane.
Things just:
HAPPEN.
And you never know --

WHAT'S --
Going to happen --
Until you --
WATCH IT --
Happening.
LIKEWISE --
You never know --
WHAT YOU'RE GOING TO DO --
UNTIL YOU --
WATCH --
YOURSELF --
DO IT.
SO:
YOU SEE:
YOU ARE:
ALWAYS:
SURPRISED.
....
There is no DESIRE on the causal plane.
The BASIC PREMISE --
Of the causal plane is:
THE PERFECTION OF THE UNIVERSE.
Whatever is happening --
IS EXACTLY WHAT IS SUPPOSED TO HAPPEN.
Whatever you DO --
IS PRECISELY WHAT YOU ARE SUPPOSED TO DO.
Whatever anyone ELSE does --
IS PRECISELY WHAT *THEY* WERE SUPPOSED TO DO.

It is only the EGO --
That labels things:
Good or bad.
Right or wrong.
THERE IS NO EGO ON THE CAUSAL PLANE.
On the CAUSAL PLANE --
EGO IS:
LONG GONE.
Even TRAGEDIES --
Or HORRIFIC ACTS OF VIOLENCE --
Are seen as:
EXQUISITE AND NECESSARY EXPRESSIONS --
OF ALL THAT IS.
All That Is --
EXPLORING --
AND EXPRESSING --
ITSELF.
The OPERATING PRINCIPLE OF:
ALL THAT IS --
IS:
EVERYTHING THAT CAN HAPPEN --
MUST HAPPEN.
AND HOW CAN YOU --
ARGUE --
WITH:
ALL THAT IS?
....
On the CAUSAL PLANE --

You have DISCARDED --
The lens of the EGO --
The lens of the HEAD --
For the lens of the HEART.
FORGET ABOUT --
EGOIC --
CONCEPTUALIZATIONS --
OF THE HEART.
The BOTTOM --
INESCAPABLE --
LINE --
IS THAT:
THE HEART:
LOVES --
EVERYONE --
AND EVERYTHING --
WITHOUT EXCEPTION.
THE HEART --
EMBRACES --
EVERYONE --
AND EVERYTHING --
WITHOUT EXCEPTION.
The HEART --
WILL KISS --
A COW --
OR A CHICKEN --
OR A PIG --
AS IT IS GETTING ITS THROAT SLIT --

AND SAY:
"I LOVE YOU.
YOU ARE SO BEAUTIFUL."
THE HEART --
WILL ALSO:
KISS --
THE MAN --
WHO SLIT THEIR THROAT --
AND SAY:
"I LOVE YOU.
YOU ARE SO:
BEAUTIFUL."
....
On the causal plane:
There is no SELF --
And OTHER.
There is only:
YOU.
EVERYONE ELSE --
IS JUST:
INCARNATIONS OF YOU --
SHOWING YOU:
WHO --
AND WHAT --
YOU ARE.
They are ALL:
YOUR CHILDREN.
On the CAUSAL PLANE:

YOU --
ARE AN:
OVERSOUL.
IT IS --
YOUR *JOB* --
TO LOVE --
AND EMBRACE --
ALL OF THESE:
OTHER YOUS.
IT IS:
YOUR JOB:
TO *CHEER ON* --
ALL OF THESE -
OTHER YOUS --
IN DOING --
WHATEVER --
THEY ARE DOING.
LOVE --
DOESN'T TRY --
TO CHANGE --
ANYONE.
No.
LOVE --
TELLS EVERYONE --
TELL ITS:
CHILDREN:
"YOU ARE BEAUTIFUL --
AND I LOVE YOU.

PLEASE KEEP DOING --
WHATEVER IT IS --
THAT YOU ARE --
ALREADY --
DOING."
....
Of course:
THE HEART --
LOVES THE WORLD --
AS IT LOVES ITSELF --
BECAUSE --
THE WORLD --
IS:
ITSELF.
THE HEART LOVES ITSELF.
I mean --
HOW COULD IT NOT?
ALL THAT IS --
LOVES ITSELF.
I mean --
HOW COULD IT NOT?
YOU --
LOVE YOURSELF.
I mean --
HOW COULD YOU NOT?
And you love:
ALL OF YOUR INCARNATIONS --
ALL OF YOUR CHILDREN --

NOT IN SPITE OF --
BUT *BECAUSE OF* --
EXACTLY AND PRECISELY --
WHAT THEY ARE DOING.
YOU DO --
IN FACT --
LOVE --
EVERYTHING THAT THEY ARE DOING.
I MEAN:
HOW COULD YOU NOT?
YOU ARE ALL --
SIMPLY:
ALL THAT IS --
BEING --
AND DOING --
WHAT ALL THAT IS --
MUST.
YOU --
ARE --
IN FACT:
ALL THAT IS:
FULFILLING ITSELF.
On the causal plane --
You see an EVENT --
(And *YOU* --
ARE --
AN EVENT --
AND *ALL OF YOUR CHILDREN* --

ARE EVENTS --
AND YOUR --
WORLD --
IS AN EVENT) --
Yes:
ON THE CAUSAL PLANE --
YOU SEE *ALL EVENTS* --
IN ALL OF THEIR --
INFINITE --
PROBABILITIES.
IN FACT --
IN ORDER TO REALLY --
TRULY --
COMPREHENSIVELY --
SEE --
ANYONE --
OR ANYTHING --
YOU --
MUST --
SEE --
ALL OF THEIR:
LIMITLESS PROBABILITIES --
AS A:
WHOLE.
AS A:
SINGLE EVENT.
YOUR WORLD --
IS UNDERGOING --

AN APOCALYPSE.
WHAT YOU ARE BEGINNING TO *GRASP* --
IS THAT YOUR WORLD --
IS --
BY DEFINITION --
AN APOCALYPSE.
IT ALWAYS HAS BEEN.
DEATH --
AND LIFE --
ARE SO:
INEXTRICABLY --
INTERTWINED --
IN EACH INSTANT --
EACH BREATH --
AS TO BE:
INDISTINGUISHABLE.
YOU ARE BEGINNING TO --
FACE THE FACT --
THAT YOU --
HAVE TO SEE --
IT ALL.
AND BY:
ALL --
I MEAN:
ALL.

PART FORTY-ONE

In order to DO WHAT HE DOES --

Randy needs:

PRIVACY --

And:

ANONYMITY.

THAT IS WHY YOU WILL NOT SEE HIM ON TELEVISION.

PART FORTY-TWO

Randy has found something.

When he --

LIES IN BED --

FOR FIVE HOURS --

EVERY AFTERNOON --

OR MAYBE --

AN HOUR AFTER HE WAKES UP IN THE MORNING --

AND ANY OTHER CHANCE HE GETS --

And goes:

INSIDE HIS SINOATRIAL NODE --

Just lying there:

SPARKING --

And THROBBING:

THINGS HAPPEN.

His WRITING CAREER --

Is BURGEONING.

Clearly his:

MEDITATION PRACTICE --

Is BURGEONING.

He was lying in bed this morning --

INSIDE HIS SINOATRIAL NODE --

SPARKING --

And CONTRACTING --

And he noticed:

THE MUSCULAR CONSTRICTION --
WHICH HAD BEEN --
GRIPPING --
HIS HEART --
WAS GONE.
While still in bed --
He wrote his massage therapist Jody --
And told her:
"MY HEART WAS IN A CAGE.
NOW IT IS FREE --
TO FLY."
....
We mentioned the NEW --
SILVER PLATTER --
BEARING GIFTS --
APPEARING ON THE HORIZON --
HEADING --
ON THAT CONVEYOR BELT --
STRAIGHT FOR:
RANDY AND GAVIN'S:
LAPS.
Well.
It is HERE.
There is an astral:
SAUSAGE GRINDER.
This SAUSAGE GRINDER --
GROUND UP --
RANDY AND GAVIN'S:

LOVE --
SUCH AS IT WAS --
IN ALL ITS TENDERNESS --
SILLINESS --
AND:
OUT-OF-WHACKNESS.
THEN *SPIT IT OUT* --
RECONFIGURED --
MOLECULE BY MOLECULE.
Mostly what got *PURGED* --
Was the PLETHORA --
Of ANTIQUATED --
CONCEPTS --
CONCEPTUALIZATIONS --
CATEGORIZATIONS.
WRONG-HEADED --
AND CRIPPLING --
EXPECTATIONS.
CAGINGS.
ALL OF THAT IS GONE NOW.
NOW:
THEIR LOVE:
IS FREE:
TO FLY:
AND BE:
THE MIRACLE:
THEY WERE:
WITH ALL THEIR GOOD INTENTIONS:

KEEPING:
IT FROM:
BEING.
And now:
LOOK AT THAT LOVE FLY!
THROUGH --
CLEAR EMPTY --
SKIES --
OF LIGHT --
AND JOY.
WATCH IT --
DIVE DEEP --
INTO OCEANS --
TSUNAMIS --
OF LOVE.
WATCH IT --
PENETRATE --
BLACK --
STAR-TWINKLED --
NIGHT SKIES --
INTO --
THROUGH --
AND *FAR PAST* --
SLEEPING DREAMS.
WHERE ONLY:
TRUE GODS --
CAN WAKE.
AND SING.

AND PLAY.
AND:
KNOW.
LET ALL TRUE --
EMISSARIES --
OF GOD --
FALL TO THE GROUND --
AND TREMBLE --
AT THE:
SPECTACLE.
……..
When you DISCOVER --
WHAT IS POSSIBLE --
YOU WILL NOT SETTLE --
FOR ANYTHING --
LESS.
You CANNOT --
PUT THAT BIRD --
BACK INTO --
THAT CAGE.
YOUR *WORLD* --
IS NOW --
ESCAPING --
FROM THAT --
SAME CAGE --
THAT RANDY'S HEART --
AND RANDY AND GAVIN'S --
LOVE --

ESCAPED FROM.
Do not be DECEIVED.
There are MANY --
BEAUTIFUL PRISONS --
IN YOUR WORLD --
AND IN YOUR MINDS --
AND IN YOUR HEARTS.
TEMPTING --
LURING --
DEADLY.
When Randy spends FIVE HOURS --
AND MANY MORE --
THAN FIVE HOURS --
INSIDE HIS:
SINOATRIAL NODE --
SPARKING --
AND CONTRACTING --
DO YOU KNOW WHAT HAPPENS?
YOUR HEART --
AND *YOUR* HEART --
AND *YOUR* HEART --
FLIES OPEN.
YOUR:
WORLD'S HEART --
FLIES OPEN.
At that point:
You will not need God --
BECAUSE YOU WILL BE:

GODS.
You will not need ETs --
BECAUSE YOU WILL BE ETS.
FLYING THROUGH SKIES --
OF LIGHT --
AND JOY.
EXPLORING BOLDLY --
ALL THE:
VAST TERRORS --
AND ECSTASIES --
OF DEEP SPACE.
PLUNGING INTO THE:
TRANSMOGRIFYING --
TEAR-DRENCHED:
SWEETNESS –
OF ONE HAND --
TOUCHING --
ANOTHER HAND.
OR A:
CAT.
KNOWING THAT THIS TOUCH --
MEANS:
EVERYTHING.
....
Once you have found this --
Once *THIS HAS FOUND YOU* --
Once --
WE --

HAVE FOUND YOU --
ONCE:
YOU --
HAVE FOUND --
YOURSELVES --
(BECAUSE THAT IS --
ALL --
THAT WE --
EVER WERE) --
YOU WILL SAY --
YOU WILL --
KNOW --
AFTER ALL THESE EONS --
YOU WILL --
FINALLY --
KNOW:
THAT YOU HAVE ARRIVED.
YOU:
ARE:
HERE.
ALL THE GODS --
WILL WEEP WITH JOY --
WATCHING EVERY DREAM --
THEY HAVE EVER DREAMED --
COME TRUE.
IN YOU.

PART FORTY-THREE

Last night Gavin and Randy were having a LOFTY discussion –

About JOY.

JOY IS SOMETHING THEY BOTH KNOW WELL –

AS WELL AS THE FULL SPECTRUM OF:

BLOOD, GUTS AND GORE --

IN YOUR FACE –

GUT PUNCH –

EVERY HORROR –

AND TERROR –

NIGHTMARE –

YOU EVER DARED TO DREAD.

Is joy "better than" terror?

Is it "preferable"?

We could have this discussion on many levels.

On the egoic level:

You want to be HAPPY ALL THE TIME –

And have EVERY DESIRE FULFILLED.

On the astral level:

EVERY JOY MUST BY WON BY THE SLAYING OF A CORRESPONDING (POLAR) DEMON.

You know those discussions well already.

Let's attempt a discussion of JOY –

FROM THE CAUSAL PLANE.

....

First of all –

On the CAUSAL PLANE –

You are already the:

SELF.

ALL THAT IS.

THE ENTIRETY OF UNIVERSE/MULTIVERSE/ OMNIVERSE/ANTIVERSE –

And the entirely of:

EACH INDIVIDUAL OF *EACH CIVILIZATION* IN ANY AND ALL OF THESE PLANES/PLANETS/DIMENSIONS/ REALMS –

THE VAST MAJORITY OF WHICH –

NEEDESS TO SAY –

ARE EXOPOLITICAL IN ORIGIN.

You are every tree, flower, raindrop, kernel of corn, grain of sand, teardrop, semen drop, quark, quasar, potbellied politician.

You are every murderer, murder victim, homeless person, racist, slaughtered cow, lynch mob, lynch mob victim, baby born, sack of kittens dropped in a river.

We've called this –

SOMEWHAT IN JEST –

The CURSE OF BEING ALL THAT IS –

"Curse" for obvious reasons –

"Jest" for reasons we will soon explore.

....

"Happy all the time" doesn't quite seem like a viable option anymore, does it.

Not from the ego/human/astral perspective.

But on the CAUSAL LEVEL –

You –

OF NECESSITY –

Must ask:

WHAT ARE THE NEEDS AND WANTS OF ALL THAT IS –

OF THE SELF –

OF THE GODHEAD –

OF THE *HIGHER ECHELONS OF WHO YOU ARE.*

Because THAT –

Is WHO YOU ARE now.

....

A brief survey here of the:

LAWS OF PHYSICS –

On the CAUSAL PLANE.

There is no desire.

There are no preferences.

There is no conception of:

Good and bad –

Right or wrong.

There is no preference –

For one outcome over another.

There is no planning.

There are no goals –

NOT EVEN "NOBLE" GOALS SUCH AS WORLD PEACE, EQUALITY, THE ALLEVIATION OF SUFFERING.

There is no effort.

There is no TRYING to do anything –

Not even to do "good" things.
There is no desire to "help" –
Because you SEE CLEARLY that:
NO HELP IS NEEDED.
And *THIS* –
Is the KICKER:
THERE:
IS:
NO:
THOUGHT.
....
On the CAUSAL PLANE –
You RELATE –
You *COMMUNITATE* –
On the level of the atoms, molecules, cells.
You know that VAST BEINGS –
I DARESAY:
GODS –
Inhabit these tiny particles.
You get down –
Into –
The:
NITTY GRITTY –
Of *WHAT REALITY IS MADE OF.*
You know –
From DIRECT EXPERIENCE –
AND NOT FROM ANY TEACHING –
NOR EVEN FROM ANY *SCRIPTURE* –

That reality –
ANY REALITY –
OF ANY REALM/PLANET/PLANE/DIMENSION –
Is COMPOSED OF:
BASIC *BUILDING BLOCKS.*
These are:
WHAT REALITY IS.
They are, of course:
Also:
WHAT YOU ARE.
They are:
WHO –
And WHAT –
EVERYONE IS.
These:
UNIVERSAL –
BUILDING BLOCKS ARE:
LOVE.
JOY.
BLISS.
LIGHT.
....
Jesus hanging on the cross –
GLOWED.
Kali and Shiva –
KILL AND CELEBRATE KILLING.
The Knights Templar –
SANG HYMNS –

AS THE FAT IN THEIR FEET –
BUBBLED IN THE FIRE.
Years ago Randy attended a fundraiser in Dayton.
A gentleman sitting at the next table GLOWED.
Randy asked his friend to introduce them.
They shook hands –
NEITHER ONE KNOWING WHY.
The next week Randy's friend called –
And told him that this gentleman –
Had dropped dead from a heart attack.

....

Randy has suffered greatly in his life.
He would say he still does.
When Randy suffers –
He HOLDS HIMSELF.
He says;
"Randy Lee Higgins, I love you.
I'm here for you.
It's OK."
Randy has learned how to be –
Not only his own BEST FRIEND –
But also:
HIS OWN GUARDIAN ANGEL.

....

You can't get away from the suffering of the world.
YOU CAN'T GET AWAY FROM BEING ALL THAT IS.
Any time you are thinking something is:
GOOD OR BAD –

RIGHT OR WRONG –

PREFERABLE OR NOT PREFERABLE –

You have slipped into ego.

AND THAT IS A DISCUSSION THAT WE ARE NOT HAVING.

THERE IS NO SOLUTION IN EGO.

THERE ARE NO ANSWERS IN EGO.

IF YOU CAN –

REMAIN –

IN A STATE OF:

LOVE/JOY/BLISS/LIGHT –

DURING A MASSACRE –

OR A TRUCK LOAD OF PIGS GETTING THEIR THROATS SLIT –

OR LOSING EVERYTHING YOU EVER HELD DEAR --

OR A *FULL-BLOWN APOCALYPSE* --

THEN YOU:

ARE A:

FULL-TIME –

RESIDENT –

AND CITIZEN –

OF THE:

CAUSAL PLANE.

PART FORTY-FOUR

It feels like the end is near.
Both of this book –
And of this world.
This one particular –
PECULIAR –
World.
A world that EVERYONE WANTED –
But that *NO ONE WILL MISS.*
That is –
IN FACT –
Your BEST KEPT SECRET:
NOBODY –
WANTS –
TO BE HERE.
But you know what?
THAT IS A GOOD SIGN!
IT IS A GREAT SIGN!
A SIGN OF GLAD TIDINGS!
Earth is associated with a --
CLUSTER:
Ego development –
WHICH WAS NECESSARY.
Karma and reincarnational dramas –
WHICH WERE NECESSARY.

Religious systems that –
HINT –
And TEASE.
That take you a *MILLIMETER OR TWO* –
Closer to WHO YOU ARE –
But then CONDEMN YOU TO DEATH –
If you actually –
DARE TO BE.
Necessary?
Perhaps.
In the most GENERIC –
PROPHYLATICALLY –
AMELIORATIVE –
Sense.
Let's say it was the SLIMMEST BEGINNINGS –
Of a kind of INFANTILE –
PRECURSORY:
CONSCIENCE.
We will grant the HINT –
Of a HYPOTHETICAL –
SYMBOLIC –
BABY STEP.
Religion told you that there was:
MORE THAN MET THE EYE.
Pity they couldn't even *REMOTELY* –
SHOW YOU WHAT THAT WAS.
Randy CRACKED THAT EGG –
With Seth –

When he was sixteen.

That was when he went to a FIELD –

And found a ROCK –

And:

SAT.

NOTHING IN THE OUTER WORLD –

CAN BRING YOU TO THE INNER WORLD.

NOTHING.

Not religion –

Not teachers –

Not drugs.

No.

You are in PLATO'S CAVE.

AS LONG AS YOU ARE CHAINED UP –

STARING AT THE SHADOWS ON THE WALL –

(Those shadows being ANYTHING AND EVERYTHING IN THE OUTER WORLD –

INCLUDING RELIGIONS, TEACHERS, DRUGS) –

You are HELPLESS –

HAPLESS –

HOPELESS.

YOU –

Have to BREAK THE CHAINS –

And TURN AROUND –

And WALK OUT OF THAT CAVE –

INTO THE SUNLIGHT.

....

Continuing with that analogy –

YOUR WORLD –

IS –
THE BACK OF THAT CAVE.
YOUR WORLD –
IS:
ALL THOSE SHADOWS.
Ego.
Religion.
Teachers.
Drugs –
EVEN THE GOD DRUGS OF PSYCHEDELICS.
IF YOU THINK –
THAT YOU CAN "GET THERE" –
THROUGH *ANY* –
EXTERNAL MEANS –
THEN YOU ARE:
STILL:
HELPESSLY –
HAPLESSLY –
HOPELESSLY –
CHAINED IN THAT CAVE.
....
The GOOD NEWS is that:
YOU ARE STEPPING OUT OF THAT CAVE.
EARTH –
IS THAT:
CAVE.
YOU ARE STEPPING OUT OF:
EARTH.

HALLELUHAH!
THERE IS HOPE AFTER ALL!
BUT ONLY –
IF YOU:
STEP OUT OF:
THAT CAVE.

POSTSCRIPT

The fact of the matter is:
ONCE YOU STEP OUT OF THAT CAVE –
AND WALK INTO THE SUNSHINE –
THAT CAVE IS STILL THERE.
BUT IT DOESN'T MATTER.
IT BECOMES COMPLETELY IRRELEVANT.
ALL YOU KNOW:
IS THAT YOU ARE NEVER SETTING FOOT –
INSIDE THAT CAVE AGAIN.
....
BUT WON'T YOU –
WANT –
TO GO BACK IN –
TO FREE –
ALL THE OTHER PRISONERS –
OF EARTH?
NO.
NOT AT ALL.
BECAUSE THAT IS A:
CAVE OF SHADOWS.
YOU CAN ONLY GO BACK IN THERE –
AS A:
SHADOW.
THUS MERELY –
PERPETUATING THEIR MISERY.
"LET ME HELP YOU WITH YOUR PROBLEM" –

ONLY DIGS THE PERSON –

DEEPER STILL –

INTO THE PROBLEM.

The INNER COUNCILS are strict.

The *PRIME DIRECTIVE* is:

INVIOLABLE.

Meaning:

YOU COULDN'T VIOLATE IT IF YOU TRIED.

WHAT DO YOU THINK WOULD HAPPEN IF YOU TRIED TO HELP A BUTTERFLY –

OUT OF ITS CHRYSALIS?

YOU LAUGH –

BECAUSE YOU KNOW –

THAT THE:

INTELLIGENCE OF THE UNIVERSE:

KNOWS WHAT IT IS DOING.

....

YOU ARE A SUN NOW.

YOU ARE THE BLACK HOLE AT THE CENTER OF THE GALAXY.

YOU ARE NOW:

THE GODHEAD ITSELF.

AS SUCH:

YOU HAVE NO DESIRE.

YOU HAVE NO THOUGHT.

YOU HAVE NO PLANS.

YOU HAVE NO AGENDAS –

INTERGALATIC OR NO.

THE UNIVERSE/MULTIVERSE/OMNIVERSE/

ANTIVERSE –
IS:
PERFECT.
EACH SPARROW FALLS –
SO EXQUISITELY –
FROM THE SKY.
YOU –
AND ALL –
ARE ONE.
LIFE –
AND DEATH –
ARE ONE.
ALL IS ACCEPTED –
LOVED –
EMBRACED –
CHERISHED –
FORGIVEN.
EVEN THE UNFORGIVABLE.
YOU HAVE LEARNED –
TO *LOVE:*
THE UNLOVABLE.
....
AND FOR THAT:
YOU ARE GREATLY REWARDED.
AS YOU LEAVE:
THE PLAYGROUND.